£6-00

METALWORK

A Companion to "Metalwork"

OLD FURNITURE AND WOODWORK

An Introductory Historical Survey

By Donald Smith

This Book, which is aimed principally to provide the historical background for the student woodworker, traces the evolution in the various uses of wood in furniture from the earliest times to the present day. Lavishly illustrated from drawings by the author and from numerous photographs of historical examples.

*

"The numerous illustrations, photographs and sketches, and the text go together and provide an excellent incentive for the study of furniture itself."
—*The Times Educational Supplement.*

*

"Woodwork is the first book on its subject designed purely for school use, and is indispensable to teachers." —*The Schoolmaster.*

*

"It traces the evolution of each piece of furniture from the earliest times and succeeds in making the story extremely interesting. A list of "Things to Do" is given at the end of each chapter and the illustrations and plates are excellent." —*A.M.A.*

*

"Unusual is perhaps the most fitting word to apply to this book, but one would hasten to add, fascinating also. It deals with one medium (wood), hence the title, and it tells the life-story of some of the more important kinds of furniture and their development through the ages. It is evidence of wide study and careful observation. The text is interesting and the illustrations are not only well chosen but reproduced very satisfactorily."
—*Journal of Education.*

DEMY 8VO · · SECOND EDITION

A BATSFORD BOOK

A Prehistoric Bronze Shield, ornamented with enamelled
bosses. Found in the Thames at Battersea and now in
the British Museum.

METALWORK

An Introductory Historical Survey

by

DONALD SMITH

Author of
"Old Furniture and Woodwork"

B. T. BATSFORD LTD.

LONDON – NEW YORK
TORONTO – SYDNEY

FIRST PUBLISHED, *Spring 1948*

Made and Printed in Great Britain by
Messrs. Balding & Mansell Ltd., London and Wisbech
for the Publishers, B. T. BATSFORD, LTD.
LONDON: 15 North Audley Street, W,1. and Malvern Wells, Worcestershire
NEW YORK: 122 East 55th Street
TORONTO: 480 - 6 University Avenue

CONTENTS

Acknowledgment

The Publishers have pleasure in acknowledging their obligation to the Museums and Photographers who have co-operated in supplying the photographs from which the illustrations in this book have been reproduced, namely:—The British Museum, for Plates I, III (1, 2 and 3), XIII (2) and XV (1); the late Brian C. Clayton, for Plates X (1 and 2) and XXI (1 and 2); Herbert Felton, F.R.P.S., for Plate XX (3); Messrs. Horton, Bristol, for Plate XX (4); A. F. Kersting, F.R.P.S., for Plate X (3 and 5); Messrs. London Electrotype Agency, Ltd., for Plate XII (2); Messrs. Musto, for Plate IV; The National Museum of Ireland, Dublin, for Plate XIII (3, 4 and 5); The Schlossmuseum, Berlin, for Plate XIII (1); Sigmaringen Castle Museum, Germany, for Plate XI; The Times Publishing Co., Ltd., for Plate XV (1); The Victoria and Albert Museum, London, for Plates VIII (1), XV (2), XVI (1, 2 and 3), XVII (1 and 2), XVIII (1, 2, 3 and 4), XIX (2) and XXII (1 and 2); and The Wallace Collection, London, for Plate XII (1 and 3). The remainder of the illustrations are from photographs in the Publishers' own collection.

CHAPTER ONE

The Dawn of Metalwork

THERE is a great difference between the way in which man makes things of wood, and the way in which things are made of metal. The woodworker deals with a vegetable fibre. His raw material, timber, was a growing thing composed of millions of living cells forming the trunks or branches of trees. He takes blocks or planks of this raw material and makes the thing he wants by removing the surplus or waste wood by the use of cutting tools. In the same way the stone mason takes his raw material, the block of stone, and removes the waste and so reveals the shape he needs. The substance of the wood that is left in the finished portion has not been changed. If it was not well seasoned a little more sap might dry out, but that is all. An old story tells how Michael Angelo visited a quarry and standing before a block of roughly shapen marble said that he could see an angel in it. In the same way, every true woodworker can see in the piece of wood on the bench the object he has to make. He has but to cut away the waste.

The raw material of the metal worker comes from the earth, it never had life, it is a mineral. In most cases it has already suffered great changes before it comes to his hand. In almost every case it has been subjected to great *heat* during its extraction from the ore. It has had a physical change by being smelted, and has been liquified in order to be shaped into ingots, bars or sheets, etc., so that it can be easily handled. Very often it has had its nature changed by the addition of other metals or substances. A little carbon changes a soft iron to a hard steel. By mixing small quantities of one or more other metals a metallic mixture called an alloy is made. The addition is usually made, either to harden a soft metal such as gold, or silver or copper, or to change its colour. The alloy is sometimes so different as to receive a new name, i.e., brass is copper and zinc, bronze is copper and tin, pewter may be tin and lead, or tin and copper or tin and a number of other metals. The important matter to notice is that in every instance man has to call *fire* to his aid.

When the metal *is* ready for the craftsman it is shaped mainly by two methods. It is either melted again and poured into moulds, or it is beaten into shape by hammers.

The principal tools of the metal worker are the FURNACE and the HAMMER.

THE FURNACE. It is interesting to notice that the words 'smith and smithy', 'hammer', 'hearth' and 'bellows' are Anglo-Saxon words, while 'furnace', 'founder or foundry' and 'forge' are old French words, indicating that while the smith carried on with his work for long before the Conquest, the business of smelting ores was established after the Normans came.

A furnace needs two things, fuel and a forced draught. For long ages the fuel used was wood, or wood prepared as charcoal. Even charcoal burns quickly, and this added to the great difficulty of obtaining enormous quantities, prevented the metal worker from handling really large work. The use of coal, which is very recent, has made possible the handling of huge masses of metal.

The first furnace no doubt was formed by man supplying the blast from his mouth, as we do to quicken a slow-lighting fire, or when using a blow-pipe for fine soldering. Primitive forms of bellows however, are of great antiquity. ('Bellows, belly and bag' are all derived from the same Anglo-Saxon word, of which 'bag' gives the best meaning.) The first bellows, which also gave the first forced draught and the first valve consisted no doubt of an animal skin fitted with a hollow bone nozzle and having a hole as an air inlet which could be closed by pressing down with the hand. Two of these bellows worked alternately by the hands of a slave would give a fairly continuous blast of one-man-power. Legs are stronger than arms, and the earliest known representation of a mechanical means of producing a blast is to be found in an Egyptian tomb dating from at least 1500 B.C. This wall painting shows two large flat earthen pots covered with skins. Each skin had a central hole which was closed by the heel of the workman who stood in the pots slowly 'marking time', raising the skins in turn by cords held in his hands. A simple advance from this apparatus gave the bellows, with which we are still familiar, with its lever for use by hand or foot. Another step forward gave the double chamber bellows. This supplies a continuous blast, and is used the world over by shoeing smiths. During the Middle Ages wherever there was a sufficient fall of water, a 'water blower' or 'trompe' was often used. In recent years fans and rotary blowers have been invented that give continuous blasts of almost any power.

For many centuries the use of charcoal made it impossible to produce sufficient heat to smelt the ore thoroughly. The ore and fuel was mixed and the furnace 'charged'. After firing, the furnace was closed and the blast raised as great a heat as possible. The molten metal ran to the hollow hearth at the bottom of the furnace and when the charcoal was consumed the furnace was opened and the mass of metal, mixed with ash and impurities was removed. The metal mass was called a 'bloom' from an Anglo-Saxon word meaning a lump. These blooms were purchased by the smiths who then had the labour of hammering them into bars or sheets for their work. Later on the founders used water power for trip-hammers and supplied the raw iron in the form of bars. In the south of England there are still numerous 'Furnace Ponds', 'Hammer Ponds' and 'Forge Ponds' which tell of the old iron industry.

THE HAMMER is regarded by many as being man's first tool. Clench your fist and you have the first hammer, whether for the horizontal punch or for the vertical blow. The wooden club lengthened the reach and the length gave increased power to the blow. The 'hammer stone' of prehistoric man gave the hardness that the human hand lacked. The addition of a wood or bone haft gave the hammer itself which has remained the same through countless ages although it has taken endless shapes according to the uses to which it has been put. The metal worker uses every type, from the wooden dresser and mallets of the plumber or repoussé worker, the hide mallet of the art metal worker, the copper headed hammer of the engineer, to hammers of all shapes and sizes, from the tiny ones used by jewellers and watchmakers to the sledge of the Blacksmith. (Sledge is derived from the same Anglo-Saxon word that gives us 'slay', meaning to beat or strike. It is interesting that the small iron mace or club was revived in the first Great War for trench fighting. Mallet is derived from the other side of our word family. It is from the latin 'malleus' a hammer. A maul or mall is a large wooden hammer and a mallet a small one.)

The different ways by which things are made of metal, wood or stone have been mentioned. These different methods depend upon the different natures or qualities of the raw materials. The important properties which distinguish metals from timbers or stones are these.

(*a*) Metals can be softened or melted by heat, and when cooled will reharden and retain the shapes they were given when soft or melted. They are FUSIBLE and can be CAST.

(*b*) Metals can be hammered into shape, either when they are cold, or when they are heated. They are MALLEABLE.

(*c*) Metals can be drawn or bent to desired shapes or wire either when hot or when cold, and will retain those shapes. They are DUCTILE.

(*d*) Metals can be joined together by means of heat, either with or without another metal (a solder). They can be WELDED, SOLDERED, BRAZED or 'BURNT' together.

There are exceptions to all these statements; at ordinary temperatures Mercury is a liquid; Lead cannot be drawn into wire. Some metals are too soft to be soldered or brazed.

It is important to bear in mind the ways in which the metal worker joins the different parts of his work together. If the articles can be cast, or 'struck' or forged in one piece (a bell, or a coin or a horse-shoe) the problem does not arise. The woodworker makes a joint, or he nails, pegs or glues. The metal worker may join by lapping the edges of thin sheets together, as does the tin-smith, he may rivet his pieces together in various ways, he may weld or burn, or solder together, he may use a threaded bolt, or he may even screw or nail his metal to a core of wood or other substance.

THINGS TO DO

1. Get, if you can, a notebook which is interleaved with blank pages. It should be as large as possible. Best of all, although somewhat expensive, are the loose-leaf ring folders. There can then be a section for notes, a section for drawings and sketches, a section for press cuttings, etc.

2. Note carefully all the words that are new to you. Look them up in a good dictionary or encyclopædia. Even words that are quite familiar have often most interesting derivations and connections, as, for instance, the relation between the blacksmith's sledge hammer and the words slay and slaughter.
   What is meant by a coin being 'struck', or by 'burning' metal together?

3. Look up in a good encyclopædia the articles on 'furnaces', 'bellows', 'blowing machines'. Make drawings from the illustrations.

4. Examine your bicycle pump, a kitchen bellows, a painter's blow lamp, a primus stove, a mouth blow-pipe, the brazing equipment of the manual room. Inspect if you can a blacksmith's bellows, a portable forge.

5. Make a model of a primitive bellows, or of a water-blower (a trompe), or of an electric fan.

6. Start a series of drawings of hammers, giving the size and weight of each as far as is possible, and a note as to its use. This may lead to steam hammers, pile drivers, mechanical riveters, and percussion tools of all kinds, but that will not matter.

7. Make specimens of as many of the methods of joining two pieces of metals as possible. Try your hand on all kinds of metals. If your manual room does not possess facilities you can usually see brazing and welding done at the local garage or blacksmiths.

CHAPTER TWO

The Beginnings

WE do not know when man first began to use metal. Compared with the long ages during which men used wood and stone, metal is a very late comer. It seems that nuggets of raw gold or copper were picked up first. Their rarity and strange appearance caused them to be worn, just as amber, shells, teeth, etc., were for decoration. The mystery as to their origin aroused a feeling of awe and they were used as charms or amulets. Then some day in the dim past a fire was perhaps banked with lumps of rock and a skin-clad watcher saw with wonder that the fire, that was already a mystery to be worshipped had the power to draw from the rock a gleaming fluid that congealed and became a new thing of wonder. It was many ages before mankind recovered from the wonder of the discovery of metal. An echo of this feeling is found in the pages of the Bible. The honour of so great a discovery was claimed by all races, and the Jews claimed the distinction for the descendant of Cain called Tubal Cain who was 'the instructor of every artificer in brass and iron.'

Among the Greeks the worship of fire and the mystery of the origin and working of metals was mingled with the worship of Hephaestus, the God of Fire and Smithying. The same god was worshipped by the Romans as Vulcan. He was cast from Heaven and fell to earth in a lightning flash. He raised forges and taught useful arts to men. His forges were supposed to lie under Mount Etna, where he made thunderbolts for the Gods and arms and magical gifts for the Heroes. He is represented as having been lame. It must be remembered that in very early days a lame child or a disabled man could only survive in a world of hunters or fighters because of their value as craftsmen. In the wall paintings in Egyptian tombs, dwarfs are often shown as artificers. The cobblers and tailors of English country life were frequently men of weak or defective bodies.

The Greek myths of Haphæstus and of the Athenian craftsman Dædalus who invented the axe and sail and much beside, were paralleled in the northlands, and in Norwegian and German legends the Smiths work in mountain caves or in forest depths assisted by dwarfs and accompanying their work with secret rites which often included the inscribing of mystical runes upon their work. Among the northern people the skill of the smith was held in high honour, and among the accomplishments of King Olaf is stated . . 'he was . . *very exact and knowing in all kinds of smithwork, whether he himself or others made the thing.*' The Bible puts a high honour upon workers in metal.

Bezaleel and Aholiab, "*filled with the spirit of God, and in understanding and in knowledge, and in all manner of workmanship, to devise cunning works, to work in gold, and in silver and in brass,*" can be read about in Exodus. "*And King Solomon sent and fetched Hiram out of Tyre. He was a widow's son . . . a worker in brass: and he was filled with wisdom and understanding, and cunning to work all works in brass.*"

The full details of the wonderful work of these craftsmen are given with a loving exactness in Exodus and Kings. The two patron Saints of metalworkers are Saint Eloi in France and Saint Dunstan in England.

The mystery that surrounded the labour of the metalwork craftsman continued to our own day in some native races. A tribe of northern Rhodesia were skilled smelters of iron. "The people believe it would be impossible to smelt iron without the medicines which they say transform the ore into iron. Consequently the principal person in connection with the iron industry is "the iron doctor", who is supposed to have jealously guarded knowledge of the different medicines. The work is only carried on in the spring. When smelting is to be done a long temporary shelter is built in which the smelters live while the work is going on. During this time they are in a state of strick tabu. They may not enter their own homes."

We must be very careful not to confuse two separate ideas. First, metalworking was mysterious and was surrounded with magic and sacred rights. Second, those crafts that were controlled by Guilds during the Middle Ages were often spoken of as 'masteries' or 'mysteries', and metalworking was included among these. The modern French word for trade or occupation is 'metier' and from its old form 'mestier' we have our words 'master' or 'mister' and 'mastery' etc.

Before giving a short history of metalworking, it will be well to think of the main uses to which metals were put which made the metal craftsmen so important.

These uses may be arranged under three headings:—

1. DECORATIVE.   2. MILITARY.   3. UTILITARIAN.

1. By DECORATIVE is meant the use of metals in the making of ornaments and of jewellery. It includes the use made of metals in the adornment of furniture, or harness, etc., or in the making of articles such as cups and trophies and of much that is called plate where such things are made mainly for show and not for use.

2. By MILITARY is meant the making of metal weapons of all kinds, of shields and armour, and in later times of all things from an eight million pound battleship (ironclad) to a Mills' hand grenade.

3. UTILITARIAN.

This section is so extensive as to require three sub-headings of its own.

(*a*) *Tools.* By tools is meant all and every appliance that is used in the making of things. The plough and farm tractor are among the farmer's tools. The needle and sewing machine are dress-maker's tools. The pen and typewriter, the compass and foot rule are tools. In this sense the blast furnace and the blow-pipe, the steel liner, the locomotive and the wheel-barrow are tools. Nor can we exclude the telephone or telegraph, or such kitchen articles as spoons or gas ovens.

(*b*) *Utensils.* By making the meaning of tools so wide the meaning of utensils becomes small. They are those things which man uses, but which do not help to make things. Cups, plates, saucers, etc., are utensils. Our knives, forks and spoons used at out meals are utensils.

This would also seem to be the best place to include the very important use of metals in the making of COINS.

Lighting appliances, candlesticks and lamps, as well as the poker and tongs on the hearth may be included here.

(*c*) *Fittings and Accessories.* Almost every other craft comes to the metalworker for assistance of one kind or another. Not only does he supply tools. The harness maker comes for buckles and studs, for rivets, stirrups and bits, the carpenter needs hinges and bolts, everyone needs nails and screws and brads. One has only to go into a really good iron-monger's shop to realise the enor-mous number of fittings and accessories the metalworker supplies to other crafts and trades.

THINGS TO DO

1. Turn back to the end of the first section and see if there is anything there which applies to this section as well.

2. Look up the stories connected with Hephæstus, Vulcan, Dædalus, the myths connected with the origin of Fire, the stories of Regin, of Wayland the Smith, of Dunstan and Eloi.

3. Never lose any opportunity of examining a tool of any kind. Satisfy your-self as to the purpose and reason for every part. Could anything about it be improved? Never weary of searching out the 'why?' of anything.

4. Take a normal room in the home and classify the metal articles contained within it.

5. Search in your local library for accounts of methods of metalworking used by primitive and backward races. You are more likely to find these in the Geographical sections than elsewhere.

PLATE II

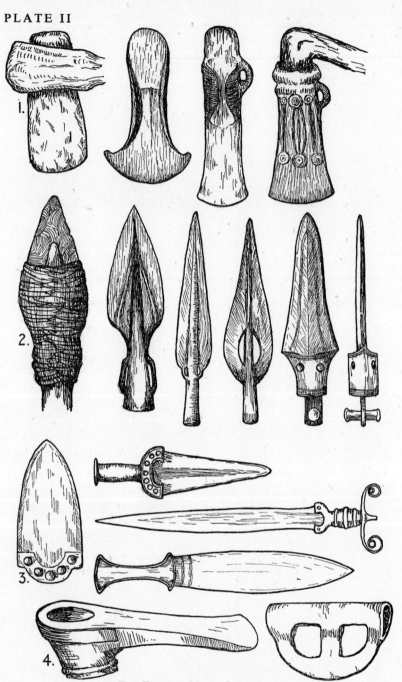

THE EARLIEST METAL IMPLEMENTS
1. Pick heads.   2. Spear heads.   3. Knives and daggers.   4. Pick heads.

CHAPTER THREE

The early History of Metalworking

FOR an incredible time mankind did without tools that were shaped; it used claw and tooth as the beasts did, or maybe took a wooden club. Then followed the ages during which stone was the principal material of which tools were made. It is usual to speak of the Old Stone Age and of the New Stone Age. Actually the Stone Age has never ceased. Until our voyagers went to the South Pacific the natives of Australia, New Zealand and the South Sea Islands had never known metal. There are still tribes in New Guinea and other remote regions who are in the Stone Age, having no knowledge of metals. Most useful little flint and steel 'lighters' are still sold for use on gas stoves. We still use a diamond for cutting glass. Every carpenter has his stone for sharpening his tools.

Gold was probably the first metal known to man. It was too soft for use as a tool maker, and so man had no Golden Age, except in myth and legend. Copper also exists in the raw state, and it separates with comparative ease from the ore, so that, here and there, there seems to have been a separate Copper Age. In Egypt copper was used first for making needles, pins, beads and bracelets, followed by chisels and cutters for drills, at the same time that the most wonderful flint implements were made and long before bronze was introduced. The Egyptians had some lost process for hardening copper, just as later on they had for hardening bronze. The shaping of the stones of the Pyramids and the carving of the Sphinx show what could be done with copper chisels. Copper is still used in the making of soldering 'irons', and for engineers' hammers where iron would give too hard a blow.

Bronze, which is an alloy of copper and tin, came with the discovery of the latter metal. It is usually supposed to have been produced first in northern Mesopotamia or Persia. China is by some regarded as the birthplace of bronze. At present the question is unsolved. The discovery of a bronze statuette of a goddess during excavation at Sakkara, near Cairo, in 1937, which is dated between 4800 and 4500 B.C., upsets all previous ideas. The perfection of the casting shows that the Egyptians must have worked in bronze for long before that date. It was commonly thought that the use of bronze was adopted in Egypt sometime about 2,000 B.C. and its manufacture had passed from Western Asia to the island of Crete between 3,000 and 2,000 B.C. The great superiority of bronze over copper or stone caused its use to spread quickly wherever trade routes ran, or wherever tin could be found to mix with copper.

Copper does not cast well; it is liable to fill with air bubbles and to make flaws, it needs a sand mould, it is soft. Bronze is very fluid when molten, it casts extremely well and does not shrink much in cooling. It can be cast in a stone mould—which can be used continuously. It is hard and takes a good edge. It can be beaten into sheets.

The Cretan mariners went far afield in their search for tin. The quest was taken up by the Phœnicians. Northern Italy had tin. Northern Spain had tin. It seems that these much travelled adventurers founded Cadiz in South Spain as a depot for their traders, who were attracted to Cornwall by the knowledge that tin was to be obtained there. There is great doubt with regard to many early dates, but it can be said perhaps that the earliest use of metal in Britain dates back to about 2,000 B.C.

It must be remembered that when Bronze did arrive on the scene human craftsmen had already acquired great skill: they could weave and carve, draw and paint, they could build and make boats, they were skilled potters, they made flint and stone implements of extraordinary finish. It is no matter for surprise that workmen were found who quickly mastered the processes of using the new material. These involved charcoal burning, the smelting of ores, the making of moulds as well as the actual casting process. Moulds were made of stone, clay, sand and of bronze itself. The first bronze implements were copied from stone implements in common use. These had been in use for long years and their shapes were good. The stone axe which is usually termed a 'celt' and which has nothing whatever to do with the people called Kelts, is commonly used as an example showing how stone shapes were copied and gradually improved by the metal casters. We say that metal is *plastic*, it can be shaped in ways impossible to stone. The first great discoveries of the metal workers was the production of a *socket* by which the shaft or haft of the tool or weapon could be affixed firmly to the head. This was done first by turning side flanges over. But about mid-way through the Bronze Age some genius hit upon the method of moulding around a core. This was one of the revolutionary discoveries of the world as it was the beginning of the casting of hollow objects. The honour of the discovery of true hollow casting was claimed by the Ancient Greeks for two sculptors of Samos, an island in the Aegean, whose names were Theodorus and Rhœcus, living in the middle of the 6th century. B.C. True sockets could now be made. The introduction of a *pin* finally enabled the maker to dispense with the cord or thong, which was a great advance. Then came the tang, and the pin became a *rivet*, and the collar and pin made its appearance. So, in those far off days, all the methods by which knives and forks, and the tools in our workshops are fastened to their handles were known and perfected. The more we consider handcraft and the tools we use the more we understand how little these things really change with the passage of time.

The first knives and daggers were probably the same implement used both for edge and point. (*See Plate II.*) It was only with experience that the knife was specialised with one cutting edge, and the dagger became mainly a point. When the dagger was bound to the end of a shaft the spear was evolved. "The Penobscot Indians say that formerly when they attacked a bear they lashed their knives to the ends of their canoe poles." When the dagger was bound at right angles to the shaft the weapon became a halbert or halberd. The lengthened dagger with a broad blade became the famous Roman thrusting sword. Developed as a lengthened point only it became a rapier. In both the broad and the long form after long ages it was affixed to rifles in the form of bayonets. The lengthened dagger which preserved its cutting edge became a true sword, which took innumerable forms.

Weapons were by no means the only product of the bronze founder. He made shields, bucklers and tools in great variety. Gouges, chisels, pins, tweezers, awls, tongs, blast-nozzles, sickles, razors, hammers, saws, fish hooks, anvils, adze-heads were some only of his stock in trade. Domestic utensils also, bowls, buckets, ewers and similar vessels were produced.

It has been mentioned already that gold was discovered before bronze was made, and as the metal workers' skill increased, so gold was used more and more. Studs and buckles for clothing, bracelets and neck-rings were made in large numbers. The neck rings are called 'torcs' and were often made of twisted metal. In the north of Europe it became extremely common to carry personal wealth in the form of rings (for arm, neck or ankle). Chieftains rewarded merit or bestowed gifts upon honoured guests in the form of gold rings. An open-handed master was praised as a 'ring giver'. It is also likely that small gold rings were used as money.

Before carrying on with the metal work of the Bronze Age it is necessary to consider the introduction of Iron. It should not be forgotten that all America knew nothing of Iron until Columbus opened the way—and that it was I R O N that enabled the Spaniards to beat the Aztecs and Incas, who only had copper and gold. The Chinese in their south-west provinces may have been the first to use iron, even as early as 3,000 B.C. Its use in India may be almost as old as in China. Nearer home we must turn once more to Egypt. There it was known almost as soon as copper. Like gold, it was regarded as a sacred or luck bringing metal. It was called 'the metal of heaven' and their myths speak of the heavens as being an enormous iron plate. In the same way the Mesopotamians called it the 'heaven stone'. This is probably due to the fact that the first knowledge of iron was gained from its meteoric form and that the meteor, which apparently dropped from heaven, was the first source of supply. Egyptian tomb paintings show iron as blue which is the colour still used in engineering drawings. In Egypt iron came into general use about 1,200 B.C., but there was a long overlapping period during which both iron and bronze were used. It was during this transition period that the very finest bronze work was produced. The British Museum 'Guide to the Antiquities of the Early Iron Age' has a coloured plate of a bronze shield as its frontispiece. (*See Plate I.*) The Assyrians were skilled workers in bronze plate. It is stated that they even armoured the whole circuit of town walls with sheet metal. It may be that they were the first to sheathe or to cast gates and doors of bronze. At Nineveh and Babylon they erected colossal statues. "Nebuchadnezzar the king made an image of gold, whose height was threescore cubits". A cubit is the length of the forearm from elbow to tip of the third finger. The Hebrew cubit was about $17\frac{1}{2}$ inches, so that Nebuchadnezzar's image was $87\frac{1}{2}$ feet high. This seems improbable until it is compared with the supposed size of enormous statues, some of ivory and gold, and others of bronze by the Greek sculptor Phidias. These images were built up of sheet metal. Both Assyrians and Greeks were most skilful in bronze 'repoussé', the method by which the decoration is raised by punches while the metal is supported on a bed of pitch. The pitch (mixed with tallow and resin) gives to the metal, but prevents it from cracking under the blow. Some of the Greek bronze repoussé has never been equalled by later work.

Whether this early Greek skill spread northwards we cannot truly say. We do know that at a place called La Tène, which is on the shores of Lake Neuchatel in Switzerland there developed a distinct form of decoration of bronze metal work based upon circles and flowing scrolls. This method of decoration spread northward. The people we call Ancient Britons invaded these islands in three waves, the first about 1,000 B.C. the second between 300 and 200 B.C. and the last 100 B.C., not so long before the Romans made their first attempt. These tribes brought with them the perfected method of 'Celtic' bronze work and passed it on to Ireland and Scotland. (*See Plate III.*)

The ornamentation of metal by affixing brightly coloured fragments of coral, amber or glass went before the invention of enamel. True enamel, which is made by melting (fusing) certain mineral substances on a metal ground giving a glassy (vitreous) surface, has nothing to do with the paint called enamel. The word enamel together with the modern French form émail comes from an old Teutonic word 'smaltjan' meaning to melt or smelt. We do not know when or where enamelling was first practised. The first method used was to score the metal with groves to give a hold to the fused glass. The great invention by which the metal was scooped into shallow hollow beds for the enamel, giving a sharp edge to the design probably originated in Britain, and by far the best work was produced by Celtic 'British' workmen before the Romans came.

After the Romans had gone a new kind of bronze work came to

these islands with the Saxons and the many tribes of Northmen from over the North Sea. The use of iron, particularly for weapons had reached the north, but the non-rusting and golden hued bronze was the favourite for ornaments and for articles for which the rarer gold and silver was not available. Especially on the Baltic Island of Gotland the making of brooches and sword hilts, bowls and rings developed to a wonderful extent. And so, after the Romans left, the British or Celtic skill in metalworking did not return from Ireland to which it had been driven, but the Saxons introduced their own kind of work and we have the Anglo-Saxon style. This developed best after Christianity had been introduced and workmen could live in peace within or near to the walls of churches and monasteries. Anglo-Saxon work was influenced by three separate sources:

(a) By northern work, because the workmen were by birth descendants of 'northmen',

(b) By Christianity, because the workmen lived mainly under the protection of the church, and very largely worked for the church,

(c) By the work of the south (Italy and Constantinople) because Christianity was introduced largely by monks from Rome, and it was a common practice for high church officials to travel to Rome and to bring back, not only ideas of what they had seen, but also skilled craftsmen whose work was seen and copied.

Bronze was however losing its position and by the end of the Saxon time had finally yielded to its conqueror, iron.

THINGS TO DO

1. Read and MAKE NOTES about the Bronze Age in any good history book. Get if you can, the British Museum Guides to the Antiquities of the Bronze and the Early Iron Ages. Your local library will be pleased to supply information as to books containing reference to copper, bronze, tin, iron, etc. Even when the writing is difficult the illustrations are often good.

2. Visit any museum and study the flint and bronze collections. Museum curators are usually very helpful and do not mind being asked questions. If they find that you are really interested they will often go to a lot of trouble to show you their treasures.

3. Add drawings of bronze tools, ornaments, utensils to your collections of classified drawings, making a note of their place or country.

4. Make sure that your Geography is clear. Locate place names in your reading, i.e., in this section, New Guinea, Mesopotamia, Persia, Egypt, Crete, Phœnicians (Tyre, Cadiz), Samos, the Aegean, Nineveh, Babylon,

La Tène, Gotland (the island), Rome. *Exact* knowledge prevents confused thinking.

5. Note the people mentioned, both nations (or tribes) and individuals, and look them up. For instance, Phidias the Greek will lead you to a knowledge of Greek metalworking, Hiram of Tyre to the wonderful descriptions of metal work in the Bible, etc.

6. Practise the art of 'moulding'. Old lead toys, tin soldiers, or ordinary solder easily melt in an iron spoon over a gas jet or the kitchen fire. (Be sure the spoon is iron or it may melt itself.) Paper weights, draughtsmen or chessmen, knobs for drawers, etc., are simple to cast.

7. Simple enamelling is possible wherever there is a blow pipe. Many schools have a brazing hearth, and some an enamelling oven. House and club buttons, badges, little discs, etc., for letting into decorative metal work, brooches, buckles are not difficult.

8. Repoussé work in sheet metal is a most delightful craft, either for profit or pleasure. For pleasure, a start can well be made with copper brooches of the large Scandinavian type. Delightful shapes are offered by bronze bowls, etc. A collection of the silhouettes of old bowls, vases, etc., will lead to the forming of good taste in such things.

PLATE III

1. Decoration on a prehistoric Sword Scabbard found in the River Witham (La Tène period).

2. Repoussé Horses on a prehistoric Bucket found in a cemetery of the Belgæ at Aylesford, Kent (circa 75 B.C.).

3. "The Siege". Ancient Assyrian repoussé decoration on the bronze Gates of Shalmanezer.

C

PLATE IV

The Village Blacksmith. The smith working his bellows at Manningtree in Essex.

CHAPTER FOUR

The Blacksmith

"But Iron—Cold Iron—is master of them all." Kipling.

MOST people know the old legend that tells how the craftsmen who were engaged in building the Temple quarrelled as to which was the most important. Solomon called them before him. He questioned each as he came as to who made his tools. All returned the same answer. "The Smith." Solomon sent for the smith. He came, hot from the forge, with hammer and tongs in his hand. Solomon asked him who made his tools. The smith replied, "I must e'en made my own". Then Solomon placed the Smith upon his own royal throne, for, he said, the smith was King of all the craftsmen.

We still live in the Iron Age.

Just as the word 'wright'—which comes from a Saxon word meaning 'to work'—became a general name for all who worked in wood, the ship and mill wright, the cart and wheel wright, etc., so 'Smith'—an Anglo-Saxon word, that has remained unchanged in meaning and sound—became a general name for all who work in metal, the blacksmith, the tinsmith, the goldsmith, coppersmith, silversmith, etc. Every person who wishes to make a thorough study of metalworking should first visit a blacksmith's forge, if possible, a village smithy where general work is undertaken, especially if the business is run in connection with a wheelwright as well. (*Plate IV.*) Inspect first the raw material This is mainly in the form of rods (with circular section) and bars (with rectangular section). Then inspect his equipment. In the main this has remained unchanged since the beginning. The old leathern bellows may have been displaced by a mechanical blast, and the fuel is no longer charcoal. The hearth, the water trough, the anvil, the hammer and tongs, etc., are practically as they were in the workshop of pre-historic man.

Smith's work differs from that of other crafts in that it is *wrought* work. The raw material is given a new shape *while it is hot*. The shaping is given by hammering, bending or twisting. The smith has to work swiftly, 'striking while the iron is hot'. If he hesitates, or is doubtful, or has not clearly made up his mind as to what he wishes to do, time may be wasted and the job may be spoiled. All this is reflected in his work. Good smith's work is decisive and certain. It is strong, and looks as if the smith was so sure as to what he wanted that he knew he had time enough and a little to spare. The smith also *welds*, that is, he joins two pieces of iron that have been brought to a white heat.

PLATE V

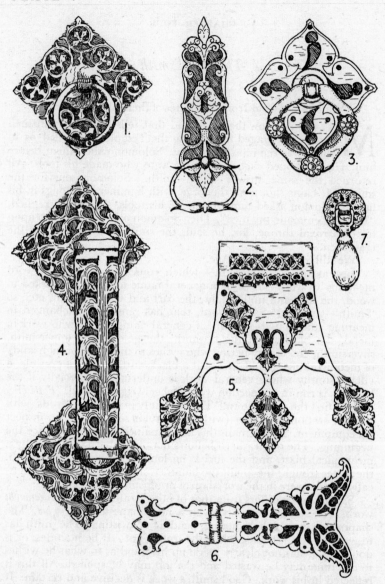

DOOR FURNITURE

1. Handle (Swiss, *c.* 1500). 2. Key-hole and handle (German Renaissance, *c.* 1650). 3. Knocker (German, *c.* 1650). 4. Knocker (Swiss, Fifteenth Century) 5. Key-hole (German, Fifteenth Century). 6. Hinge (Spanish, *c.* 1640). 7. Pendant (British, William and Mary period).

Wherever it was introduced the superiority of iron for the making of weapons and tools was unquestioned, but it could not vie with the beauty of bronze, gold or silver for ornaments. At first it was rare in Britain and so was valuable. When Cæsar came he found the Britons using long bars of iron as money. Under the Romans the forges of the Forest of Dean and elsewhere made it common enough for ordinary daily use. The fact that iron rusts so readily has resulted in the fact that remains of the bronze age are more numerous and better preserved than the remains of the early iron age.

The smith was gradually called in to assist the woodworker. After the Norman Conquest we begin to meet with specimens of smith's work,

(a) strengthening boxes and chests (*Plate VI.*)
(b) strengthening doors (*Plate VI.*)
(c) providing hinges, bolts, locks, door plates, and nails for chests and doors (*Plate V.*)

It was a time when law was barbarous and cruel, but crime was strong and violent. The safe keeping of valuable or precious things called for 'locks, bolts and bars'. From the point of view of security the wooden door was the weakest part of a building. Windows could be omitted, or placed high up, or reduced to mere slits. Even then they could be supplied with iron bars or iron grills. To strengthen the door the smith was called upon to band it, to stud it (to turn an axe's edge), or to sheathe it with iron. (*Plate VI.*) Exactly the same thing happened with the wooden chests of the time, banding and sheathing was applied until in some cases the timber itself was omitted and the thing became a metal 'safe'. The weight of the door or of the lid of the chest called for something much stronger than a wooden pin hinge, and the smith forged metal hinges. In order that these should support the door firmly they were extended across its width as 'strap' hinges. It was found that these had the additional benefit of helping to bind the timber of the door together. They were extended as the smiths gained in skill and inspiration until in some cases they covered the whole door with a network of iron. The fastening of the iron hinge to the door or chest brought the use of the nail to woodwork. The nail was most likely an adaptation of the horseshoe nail from the shoeing forge. The woodworker did not adopt the use of the nail for construction for generations except for fastening external weatherboarding, and for fixing metalwork to woodwork.

By the time that the stone mason had left the round arch and stiff decoration of the Norman building and had adopted the freedom of the pointed arch and the beauty of flowing foliage decoration, the ironworker had gained wonderful skill in designing and carrying out most intricate work on doors and chests. One wonders who was the genius who thought first of leaving out the wooden backing, leaving an independent door or screen or ironwork. It was a master thought, for it led to the making of grills, screens, rails, gates, etc. (*Plate VII.*) Of course the idea may have arisen from contemplating the iron bars closing a window opening.

The main obstacle to the constant production of ornamental ironwork has been the great usefulness of the smith in other directions. Mankind has always been troubled by wars, and the story of beautiful ironwork has long gaps which indicate that the smiths were busy making the thousands of horseshoes, arrow and spear heads, cross-bow bolts and the other munitions of war required by the long campaigns of the Middle Ages. The King always had the right to conscript labour for any purpose.

There is only room here to mention the periods which are distinguished by different kinds of smith's work.

1. THE EARLY GOTHIC. The smith, with great labour, hammered the iron blooms into flat bars. The base of his decoration was a repetition of the scroll, usually growing out from a central rib. The scrolls sometimes throw off tendrils or other scrolls, almost always from the outside curve. The smith had become skilful in the cutting of dies, and leaves, flowers, bunches of grapes, etc., were freely stamped on the hot metal. There was much punched decoration, and the bars, both of the constructional work and of the scrolls, were freely and sometimes most delicately shaped with moulding irons. Of one piece of work in this style we have details of the smith's name, the cost and the date. It is the Eleanor Grille in WestminsterAbbey and was made by 'Master Thomas de Leghtone' in 1294. We read, "by far the most magnificent piece of work of this period still left to us is the grille or grate in Westminster Abbey to the tomb of Eleanor of Castille, wife of Edward I. In it we find every detail characteristic of this manner represented in such perfection as to render the whole grille unique and unrivalled in Europe." (Ayrton and Silcock). It is very possible that these early smiths copied their designs from the lovely illuminated manuscripts of the times, or even if they did not directly copy, that they were influenced by them.

2. THE LATE GOTHIC. On the Continent there was a long late Gothic period, when smiths used the round bar or rod very greatly. Two kinds of design became common. The first was the filling of a grid of squares with the decorative shape known as a quarter-foil, and the second was the filling of shapes with a wealth of curves, spirals and flourishes which were based upon or copied from the ornate penmanship that followed the illuminated work of the monks and early writers. The spirals were formed around wooden cones which were afterwards burned out.

But in England during the fourteenth century the making of ornamental ironwork almost ceased. It was an age of wars and rebellions. It saw Bannockburn, Crecy and Poictiers; it saw the great part of the Hundred Years' War, the Black Death and the great Rising of the Villeins associated with the name of John Ball.

PLATE VI

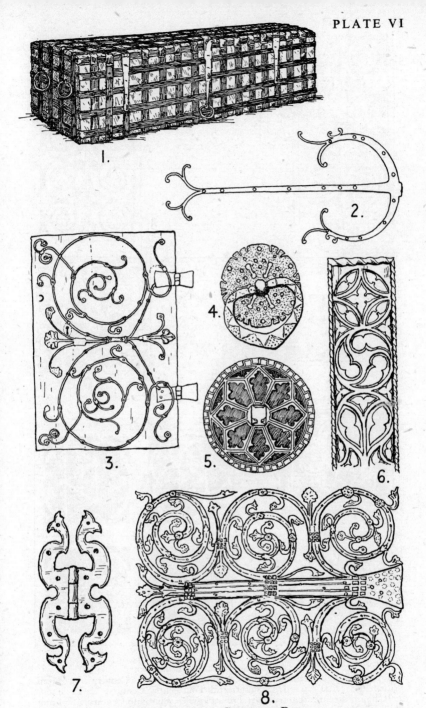

1.

2.

3.

4.

5.

6.

7.

8.

WROUGHT IRON FOR CHESTS AND DOORS

1. From Debden, Essex (Fourteenth Century).   2. From Essex (early Thirteenth Century).   3. From Chester (Thirteenth Century).   4. From Woolhope, Hereford 5. From St. Mary's, Warwick (Fourteenth Century).   6. From the Victoria and Albert Museum (Fifteenth Century).   7. Hinge (*c.* 1600).   8. Hinge (French medieval).

PLATE VII

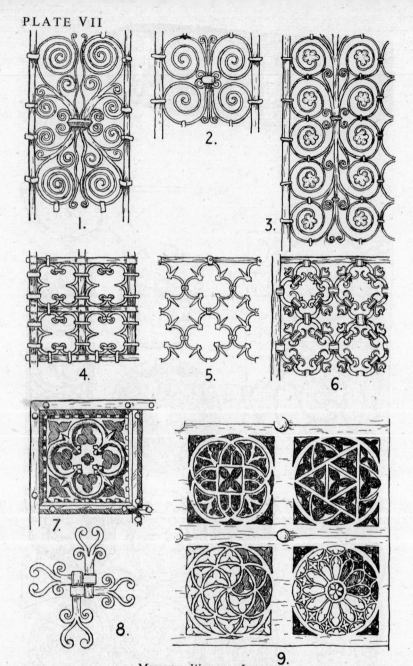

MEDIEVAL WROUGHT IRONWORK

1. French (Twelfth Century). 2. Spanish (Thirteenth Century). 3. From Winchester (A.D. 1093). 4. Thirteenth-Fourteenth Century. 5. C. 1400. 6. Italian (Fifteenth Century). 7. From Florence (Sixteenth Century). 8. From Skipwith, Yorkshire. 9. Sixteenth Century.

When the smiths were able to turn to peaceful tasks again their manner of work had entirely changed. Gone were the scrolls and flowerwork. Gone was the freedom and the delicate smith work. Everything had become geometrical and based upon the work of the stone mason. Straight-lined railings surrounded tombs and chantries. The smith and the woodworker copied buttresses and pillars, pinnacles and parapets. Especially they copied the tracery of the windows. To do this successfully the smith perfected the *piercing* of sheet metal and the use of the file. He worked largely on the methods of the locksmith and produced beautiful work for screens and for door furniture (locks, escutcheons, handle-plates, etc.) The use of the hack-saw and cold chisel, the file and the drill, made it possible for the metalworker to copy the mortice and tenon joint and other details of the woodworker. In one direction the metalworker seems to have pointed the way to the woodworker. This was in 'building up' his work by applying one piece of his detail in front of another, whereas the woodworker clung for a long time to the method of carving his detail from a solid block. Probably the finest piece of this pierced and built-up style of work is a screen and gates made for the Chantry of King Edward IV in St. George's Chapel, Windsor, by a master smith named John Tresilian in about 1480.

3. The Tudors and Stuarts. With the coming of the Tudors ornamental ironwork entered upon another bad time. The religious troubles that led up to and followed the Dissolution of the Monasteries did not encourage Church building. Then followed the long struggle between King and Parliament with its Civil War. The great consumption of charcoal for the smelting forges had caused such destruction among the oak forests of the south and west that Elizabeth repeatedly passed laws restricting the iron industry and refusing to permit the establishment of new forges. The oak was required for ship building.

4. Wren and Tijou. Not until William and Mary were invited to England in 1688 did there seem to be real opportunities for black-smiths to devote themselves to peaceable work. During the troublous times in England the blacksmiths abroad had been doing very fine work, first in south Germany and then in France. William knew of this work and when he came to England he either brought with him, or quickly sent for, a French smith of genius called Jean Tijou. This man worked in England for over twenty years, and by many people is thought to have been the most skilful of all our workers in iron. His work is based upon the use of the square bar. His mastery was so perfect that he treated iron as if it were one of the softer metals. He was first employed by the King at Hampton Court Palace. While working there he attracted the attention of Sir Christopher Wren who was enlarging the Palace for the King. Wren had travelled abroad and had studied the kind of work Tijou was doing while in France. St. Paul's Cathedral was nearing completion, and Tijou was employed upon the ironwork. It seems that Wren and he did not get on very well together, but Wren's approval would be necessary for all that Tijou suggested and carried out. Wren's common sense kept Tijou from merely showing off his wonderful skill. The ironwork at Hampton Court is fine, but the Screens, Gates, Rails and other work at St. Paul's in London have not been surpassed. (*Plate VIII.*)

5. *The Eighteenth Century* was one of the great times for wrought iron work. It was probably the greatest England has had. Peace followed the coming of William and Mary; the great prosperity of the land owners, the increasing trade of Bristol and other ports, all put wealth into the hands of the Merchants and the Gentry. The remembrance of Tijou and of the men who worked with him was fresh in men's minds, their work was there to see. It was a great time for building. Country squires, the Gentry and Nobility set about rebuilding their country houses. Copying the French plan wherever possible, they called upon their smiths to erect great and imposing screens and gates to their fore-courts and park entrances. (*Plate IX*). Ironwork reached its extreme limits in the ornate decoration of the gate panels and in the splendour of the 'overthrow', as the cresting above the gate was called. Within the house the smith was sometimes called upon to forge the superb balustrading to the grand staircase.

Within the towns the Merchants ordered gates, railings and screens for their own homes and for their favourite churches. They ordered staircases, balconies, fan-lights, and for the churches such things as font cranes, mace holders and swordrests. (*Plate X.*)

The glory of the eighteenth century ironwork came to an end not with renewed war, but by the commercial introduction of cast iron. As early as 1619 a man by the name of Dud Dudley succeeded in using coal instead of charcoal in producing pig iron. It was not until the middle of the next, the eighteenth century (at about 1757) that coal was generally used. It is strange that it should have been Sir Christopher Wren who used cast iron first for an important work. The great cast iron railings around St. Paul's are the earliest of their kind, and cost so much that Sir Christopher got into serious trouble about the matter.

Once the use of coal and the erection of the blast furnaces had been perfected, the ease and comparative cheapness with which iron could be cast drove the hand-working smith from the field. Although efforts have been made, and some fine work has been produced, the cheapness of cast work has prevented any real or general return to hand produced smith's work in the English countryside.

It would not be right to leave the blacksmith without a short reference to the enormous amount of work he does of everyday value. He is the assistant to all the crafts. So necessary is he to the wheelwright that some smiths specialise as carriage-smiths. The farmer constantly calls upon him for repairs to his agricultural implements.

PLATE VIII

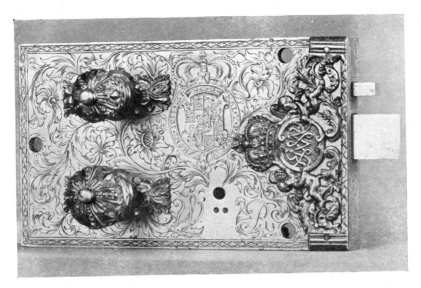

1. An engraved brass Lock with cast details, bearing the monogram of William III and Queen Mary (late seventeenth century).

2. One of the wrought-iron Side Panels by Jean Tijou (c. 1790) in the quire of St. Paul's Cathedral.

PLATE IX

Early eighteenth-century wrought-iron Gates at Belton House, near Grantham, Lincolnshire.

All ship-building, engineering and metal working firms employ blacksmiths.

The need for fastening doors and lids securely gave rise to much inventive thought. The early Egyptians made wooden locks of ingenious construction. Keys and locks of bronze have been found in large numbers at Pompeii. The KEY became a symbol of authority and office, just as the sword became the symbol of gentle birth. At the very early time of Isaiah, at least 700 years before Christ, the Key is spoken of as the emblem of Power and Judgment. Very much earlier still, shortly after the Israelites left Egypt, a door key is mentioned—in Judges 3, verse 25. The most famous of all keys are those of St. Peter which have their origin in the words of Our Lord in St. Matthew, "And I will give unto thee the keys of the Kingdom of Heaven." They appear on the coat of arms of the Pope and the Roman Catholic Church. In medieval art St. Peter is almost always represented carrying a key. The common inn signs, "The Cross Keys" or "The Keys" represent very old taverns which were built near the church in old Catholic days after the Manor House had ceased to open its doors to all comers. In the middle ages the handing over of the Keys of a Castle or town was the formal token of submission. A lady, on taking over charge of a household was formerly presented with the keys, which she wore hung at her girdle. The making of locks and keys soon became too delicate a matter for hammer and anvil. The saw, file and drill were introduced, and the locksmith became a separate craftsman. (*Plate VIII.*)

A long, long list of articles of general use made by the smith could be given. In churches one may look for hour-glass stands, chandeliers and candelabra, for font covers and cranes, for sword and mace stands. (*Plates X, XX.*) On spires and stable buildings there are weather vanes—St. Peter's crowing cock is very common. (*Plate X.*) There are brackets for Inn signs. In some cases there are old lamp brackets, and a very few link or torch holders and extinguishers. (*Plate X.*) Within doors there are a multitude of fire-side utensils and appliances, cranes and hooks for pots and kettles, fire-irons, fire dogs and irons. (*Plate XIX.*)

THINGS TO DO.

1. If possible, visit any blacksmith's shop, iron foundry, wheelwright's shop, garage, engineering works, etc., where iron work of one kind or another is being carried on. Watch how the metal is treated, note what is possible to be done.

2. After seeing *how* things are done, lose no opportunity of seeing what *has been done*. Although it is only in the larger museums that one can see specimens of important ironwork, almost all museums have quite a lot of

domestic ironwork very well worth study and sketching. Keep a sharp look out for old ironwork in old buildings of all kinds, on old wagons and vehicles. Old towns, and very often the old (and dirty) parts of town often have 'Queen Anne' or 'Georgian' houses with interesting ironwork in gates and railings, balconies, etc.

3. After seeing how things are done, and what has been done, the finest thing to do is to try *to make* something. Although the use of forge and anvil can only be had in a well equipped metalworking shop, much can be done if one has only a fairly good vice. Piercing and filing can be practiced. A great number of keyhole escutcheons, door plates, bell pushes, hinges, corner supports, etc., may be made. Riveting and bending are possible, and if there is heat enough soldering can be attempted. If there is a forge, then real smith's work can be done.

4. Continue to add to your word list, looking up the meaning of new words, and especially reading up new processes or new materials.

5. Continue your drawing. Keep separate sections for such items as Ironwork on old chests or boxes, Hinges, Other door furniture, etc.

6. Most of the books on Ornamental or Decorative Ironwork are expensive, but even if your library does not own them, it will most likely borrow them for you, although you will probably not be allowed to take them home.

7. Make a note of any great craftsman mentioned . . Thomas de Leghtone, John Tresilian, Jean Tijou. Remember the Greeks were proud of their great craftsmen.

8. Look up the wars and rebellions of the 14th century which interfered with smith's work in England.

PLATE X

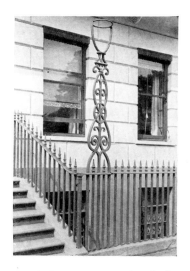

1. The Weather-vane on Sitting-bourne Church, Hampshire (1834).

2. A Regency Lamp Standard at Cheltenham, Gloucestershire.

3 and 5. Early eighteenth-century Swordrests from All Saints, Worcester, and (5) St. Giles, Cripplegate, London. 4. An eighteenth-century Lamp Standard at King's Lynn, Norfolk.

PLATE XI

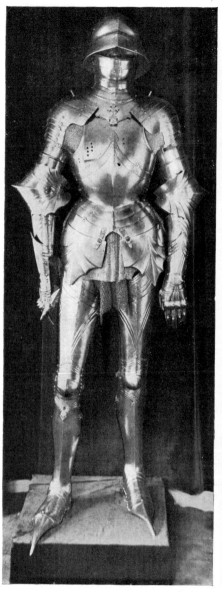

The front and rear views of a cap-à-pie suit of German Gothic Armour (*circa* 1480-1570), with its original mail-shirt. *From the Museum at Sigmaringen Castle.*

CHAPTER FIVE

The Swordsmith and The Armourer

WE have noted how the periods of war interfered with the making of decorative ironwork, because the smiths were needed to make munitions of War. When we read in the Domesday Book that the six smiths in Hereford made a yearly payment to the King of 120 horseshoes each, we know that that would not interfere with their ordinary work, but when we read of Gloucester supplying 50,000 horseshoes for Richard Cœur de Lion's Crusade in 1194 we can well understand that other work had to stand by for a time. It was not only that the smith's labour was in demand, but that the whole of the limited supply of iron was seized for the King's use. The smiths themselves were 'pressed' to the king's service unless they had the good fortune actually to be engaged on church work. It was probable, however, that, unless they were especially skilful, they were engaged in the making of spades, pickaxes, bolts, nails, wagon tyres, nave irons, chains and the host of things required by an army in the field. They might even manage arrow and spear heads, etc., but the making of the special weapons, the swords and daggers was the task of a specialist, and the making of body armour became a matter that was far above the capabilities of a general smith.

The sword came to be the most highly honoured of all weapons. It became the symbol of gentle blood. A commoner might wear a dagger, or carry a bill, but only a gentleman might wear a sword, The dignity of knighthood is conferred by a sword. Court Dress worn by high Government Officials includes a small 'dress' sword though the weapon is unused in modern warfare. Officers in the armed services in Full Dress wear swords. The sword is a gift of Kings. The Sheik of Bahrein during his visit to London in 1936 presented a gold sword to King Edward. More recently the City of London is having a sword made for General Eisenhower, and meanwhile presented him as a token with a sword of the Duke of Wellington. A sword has also been made for Stalingrad. (*Plate XX*, 2.)

Of bronze swords perhaps the most famous was the short stabbing sword—the gladius (from which we have gladiator)—of the Roman. With the introduction of iron came the added mystery of the 'tempering' of the metal. Many myths and legends surround the smithing of famous swords. . . Every boy knows the story of King Arthur's famous sword Excalibur.

> "*King Arthur's sword, Excalibur,*
> *Wrought by the lonely maiden of the Lake.*
> *Nine years she wrought it, sitting in the deeps*
> *Upon the hidden bases of the hills.*"

And all can read Kipling's story of Weland's sword in Puck of Pook's Hill: "*Then he made a sword—a dark grey, wavy-lined sword—and I blew the fire while he hammered. By Oak, Ash, and Thorn, I tell you, Weland was a Smith of the Gods! He cooled that sword in running water twice, and the third time he cooled it in the evening dew, and he laid it out in the moonlight and said Runes* (that's charms) *over it, and he carved the Runes of Prophecy on the blade.*"

And some may know of Odin's sword Gram in the story of the Volsungs, and how the smith Regin forged its broken shards anew for Sigurd, "*So he made a sword, and as he bore it forth from the forge, it seemed to the smiths as though fire burned along the edges thereof. Now he bade Sigurd take the sword, and said he knew not how to make a sword if this one failed. Then Sigurd smote it into the anvil, and cleft it down to the stock thereof, and neither burst the sword nor brake it.*"

The development of the sword followed that of armour. As the latter became more complete the sword had to become longer, stronger and heavier, until with the wearing of complete plate armour we find the enormous two handed swords that astonish us in museums today. A man could not handle these and a shield at the same time and so the guard for the hand developed, until, with the basket hilt the hand was almost entirely protected. The very highest pitch of craftsmanship was expended upon sword hilts. They were most lavishly adorned with gold, silver, enamels and precious stones (*Plate XII.*)

The making of a lighter, most highly tempered, sword arose in the East, probably in Persia, for in the hot climate the wearing of such heavy armour and wielding such heavy weapons was not possible. From Persia the making spread westwards, and Damascus became a famous home of swordsmiths. The Crusaders met with this work in Palestine. The contrast of the two is strikingly brought out in the contest of skill between Richard Cœur-de-Lion and Saladin in Scott's 'The Talisman' (Chap. 27.) The skill of the eastern craftsman was shown not only by the exquisite temper and edge of the weapon, but by the method of decoration called 'damascening'. This consisted of graving intricate patterns in the surface of the steel and of beating gold or silver wire into the hollows. The Moslems took their craft with them when they conquered Spain. The blades of Toledo and Seville became famous throughout the Continent. During the sixteenth century sword blades from north Italy named after a family of armourers, the Ferrari, became celebrated.

There was a continual competition between the makers of weapons and the makers of armour. This began in the dawn of history and continues in the 'armaments race' of today. The armourers would perfect their produce so that the wearer was safe from injury. Then the weapon maker would introduce a new and more deadly weapon . . and so the story goes on. At first a shield was sufficient, and many 'savage' races went no further. Then the

Greeks added greaves and helmets of bronze, and later on breast and back plates. The Romans added perfected shoulder guards and a sort of skirt or kilt of plates from waist to mid-thigh. The armour of the Normans appears to have consisted of a hauberk, a long tunic made probably of leather upon which small metal plates of a variety of shapes were sewn. The Bayeux Tapestry gives true pictures of Saxon and Norman armour. The plates usually overlapped like scales. This tunic, sometimes but not always lined with metal plates, was the common protection for the man-at-arms throughout the Middle Ages and was called the Jacque (Jack). A shortened variety was the ancestor of the present day jacket (jacquette). The name of the coat was transferred to the man, and we have 'jacques' as the historic nickname for the French peasant, our own 'jack of all trades', 'jack tar', etc. The remaining Norman defence was a conical head piece with a nose guard. The introduction of the long-bow from South Wales towards the end of the Norman time called for an improved armour. This was found in the general adoption of 'chain' mail, which had been known in the north for many years. This was extremely costly. The wire had to be forged, then twisted around a rod and cut to form the links. Each link had to be flattened at the ends and pierced with tiny rivet holes. The rivets had to be made. Each link had to be interlaced with other links, the ends brought to overlap and the rivet hammered in. This was the simplest kind of chain mail—each link interlacing with four others. Later on, incredible as it may seem, the links were doubled or trebled, and were welded, or else were double riveted. No wonder such suits were worth a 'knight's ransom'.

The *coat* of mail gradually extended until it covered the whole body from crown to sole, and became a *suit* of mail. The word 'mail' is derived from the latin word 'macula' one meaning of which is 'the mesh of a net'. This explains clearly the difference between the net-like mail and the later 'plate' armour. The very great risk of any exposed feature caused the armourers to produce a great variety of 'heaumes' (helms) which, with or without visors, protected the whole face or head.

The increasing weight and length of the sword, with improvements to the lance, the battle axe and mace, was met by the introduction of metal plates, first on the shoulders, and so on, until the whole body was cased in, and it is a marvel that a man could carry the woollen and padded undergarments to take the chafe and wear, then a complete suit of mail and over all a complete suit of plate. (*Plate XI.*) No wonder that the knight needed assistance in mounting his charger, that the noble beast was saved until the very last moment and resembled a carthorse, that the knight was fairly certain to come from combat unscathed, and that, if he did fall off, he would probably lie where he fell. One book on armour states, "Of course, with such a weight of armour upon him a knight when unhorsed was quite helpless, and unable to rise without the assistance of retainers."

Armour even extended from the man to the horse, until the great weight became a danger, as a fall while in action might prove fatal to both. The uselessness of such an equipment for general warfare led to its disuse. That, and the introduction of gunpowder, led to the making of lighter and lighter personal equipment. Today, although the Horse Guards wear a cuirass and helmet when on ceremonial duty, they leave these behind and wear khaki in the field. Today, when we speak of armour, we are generally referring to the plating of ships of war, or armoured cars or tanks. In the last Great War the only general use of armour by the fighting troops was the adoption of the shrapnel helmet or 'tin hat'. The armourer-sergeant in the army today concerns himself mainly with the maintenance of rifles.

The periods into which the kinds of armour can be classified simply are—

1100 - 1300.	Chain mail.
1300 - 1400.	Mixed chain mail and plate armour.
1400 - 1600.	Complete plate armour.
1600 -	Decorative armour and an ever decreasing use of plate armour.

Most firemen today when in fighting uniform wear a helmet of Greek shape and have epaulettes (shoulder pieces) of chain mail.

THINGS TO DO

1. Armour may be studied in three ways:—

    (*a*) From actual specimens. Most museums have some armour, and some museums have excellent collections.

    (*b*) from representations on church brasses. Always look and ask for old brasses when in a church. Also from *contemporary* illustrations in history books. Genuine old statues and figures on tombs have often excellent representations of armour.

    (*c*) from books dealing with armour or weapons, or with old church brasses or monuments, or books dealing with historic dress. Some Encyclopædias have good illustrated articles.

2. It is best to deal with one thing at a time, say helmets, or sword hilts. Both give a wonderful insight into the skill of the armourer. A collection of sketches of shield-shapes would be valuable and useful for design work.

3. Making puppet 'men at arms' is extremely interesting. Make first your drawings and sketches carefully from *accurate* sources. Then whittle your lay-figure from soft wood. It may be made in sections and joined together by a variety of means. Then comes the armour making: fine gauge brass, or copper, or tin plate, old coffee or cocoa tins will do. The finished 'man-o-war' makes an excellent decoration, or may be devised to hold a candle.

PLATE XII

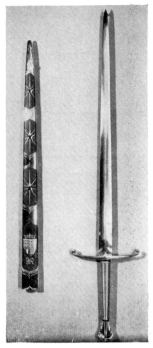

1. A highly ornamented Mace (*circa* 1560), from North Italy.

2. The Sword of Stalingrad, with its scabbard, designed by Professor Gleadowe and made in 1943.

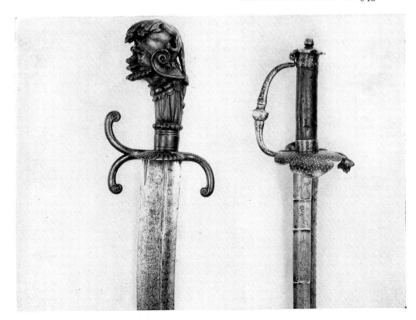

3. The Hilts of two English Swords of *circa* 1620 : to the left a "Hanger", to the right a "Falchion".

PLATE XIII

1. A highly wrought German Jewel of the eleventh century.

2. The Elizabethan Phœnix Jewel.

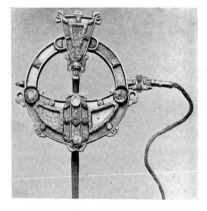

3. The Keltic-Irish Shrine of St. Patrick's Bell, and (4) the Tara Brooch.

5. The Keltic-Irish Ardagh Chalice, with its typical interlacing patterns and encrusted jewels.

CHAPTER SIX

The Goldsmith and the Silversmith

(a) JEWELLERY

THESE two words lead us to a true fairyland of craft-work. Other precious metals have been added to the list from time to time, but gold and silver reign supreme. Although they were rare they were found at places wide apart. To their rarity was added a property that gave them added value. They did not rust. When they were polished their colour and lustre had a beauty not only when standing alone, but which made an exquisite backing to precious stones and enamels. They can be worked by every method known to the metal craftsman. They can be beaten into sheets thinner than the thinnest paper and drawn into wire as thin as the silken thread. Gold can be beaten to a quarter of a million sheets to the inch, and silver to a thousand sheets to an inch. This enabled the workman from the earliest times to 'sheathe' or 'overlay', to 'gild' or to 'plate' articles made of less costly material, giving them the appearance of gold or silver and preserving them from rust or decay. Both metals can be toughened or hardened by the addition of small quantities of other metals. Their rarity and their beauty were sufficient reason for the utmost human craft-skill being expended upon them. The word 'masterpiece' may more often be given to 'jewels of gold and jewels of silver' than to any other work of man's hands.

It is difficult to write a history of the goldsmith's work. This was perfected so very long ago that there is no story to be told of a slow increase in skill as time went by. Centuries have passed, but the goldsmith today can still envy the work of the Egyptian. Of this work we read, "It is a most extraordinary fact that among them gold-work is found which not only could not be surpassed at the present day, but has rarely been equalled . . ." All that can be done is to point out the different *styles* that distinguish the work of one place and time from that of others.

Although men may have used small nuggets of gold as charms (or amulets) before the use of copper began, the softness of raw gold prevented its use for tool making, and so copper took the leading place for pure usefulness. Even before the first historic times in Egypt, that is before about 4,000 B.C., the Egyptians made gold handles for their flint knives. There seems little doubt but that gold was mined first either by the Egyptians or for them. There were two sources, first, between the Sudan and the Red Sea, and second in a region called Punt, which is supposed to have been somewhere to the south of Somaliland. Gold became extremely plentiful. As early as 1,500 B.C. it was exported to Syria, Assyria and to Babylon. Egypt seems to have been the first to use gold as money, particularly in the form of rings.

The Old Testament tells of the various uses to which gold and silver were put. Gold and a gold chain are even mentioned in Genesis. The skill gained by the Israelites while in Egypt is described in such detail as to make one guess that the writer himself must have been a craftsman. The Israelites had learned the art of gold-beating, and sheathed or overlaid much of their woodwork with gold leaf. They were masters of casting, graving, embossing and of jewellers' work. They made rings, hooks, taches, bells, cherubims, spoons, mice, altars and tables, lamps, tongs and hinges, shields, calves, basins and candlesticks, snuffers, censers, steps and footstools, ear-rings and crowns, dishes and covers, bowls and cups, and at times, idols of gold. All this great wealth of objects was made long before the coming of Christ.

In our own Islands the great source of gold and of golden objects was Ireland. The industry flourished until about 1,000 B.C. A break caused by war and invasion followed, until better times came at about 200 B.C. The Irish made armlets, bracelets, clothes studs, neck rings and a peculiar neck ornament of thin sheet gold called a lunette (*Plate XIV*). Gold rings made of twisted rods of thin bars are called torcs (or torques) from the latin 'torquere'—to twist.

Gold and Silver-smith's work will be dealt with under two head-ings, (1) Jewellery, (2) Plate. By *jewellery* is meant objects intended to be worn upon the body or carried in the hand. By *plate* is meant objects of utility made of the precious metals or covered in some way by a precious metal. Most articles of plate are intended to be stood upon some piece of furniture.

The difference between jewellery and plate is not always clear. The Bible speaks of 'jewels of gold and jewels of silver', meaning any object made of precious metal. We still speak of an official badge as being a 'jewel'. The use of the word 'jewel' as meaning a precious stone is very recent and it is far better to regard any single article, a brooch or a necklace, a casket or a bishop's crozier, as a jewel. No one knows whether jewellery was worn first as pure ornament or as charms to ward off ill-luck, or as amulets having magic powers. We all remember the magic rings of the fairy tales, and some people still wear little golden horseshoes or four-leaved shamrock. Other uses of jewels are as medals or the 'stars' of orders indicating rank or awards of honour. Jewels are worn as symbols of office such as crowns, coronets, mitres or mayors' chains; they are carried for the same purpose such as maces, staves, sceptres, processional crosses; they are worn as marriage rings to indicate personal relationship. Almost every nation has had its own special kind of jewellery. It is quite impossible to confuse Chinese with Anglo-Saxon, or to confuse Egyptian with Indian work. Experts can even tell the particular

PLATE XIV

PREHISTORIC JEWELLERY

1. Irish clothes stud. 2. Trumpet-ended bangle (Irish). 3. From a French chariot burial. 4. Brooch (from Gotland). 5. Clasp (from Desborough). 6. Sun disk (from Lansdown, Bath). 7. Enamel work (British). 8. Clasp (from Taplow). 9. Brooch (from Gotland). 10. Brooch (French).

town or region where a piece of jewellery was made, and sometimes are able to give its date.

There are many ways of making jewellery. Some is carried out in the metal by itself. The beauty of the object depends upon its shape and proportion, upon the colour of the metal and sometimes also upon the way in which patterns are worked on the surface of the metal. Sometimes two or more metals are used and their colours contrasted. Sometimes the pattern is built up of very fine twisted wire, or of very narrow bands or ribbons of metal. That is called filigree work. Some very beautiful Egyptian, Greek and early Italian (or Etruscan) work has patterns outlined with rows of very fine grains of metal. This method is used in our own famous 'King Alfred Jewel'. When the metal has been beaten into fairly thin sheets or plates it can be decorated by hammering out a pattern, using punches of various sizes—this is one form of repoussé work. Patterns can be outlined by using a tracer which has an edge like a very small cold chisel, or the pattern can be cut into the surface, when we say it has been engraved or chased. Other jewellery is cast, either as a whole, or in part.

To all these methods the worker from the very earliest time added the beauty of other coloured material, of gems and stones, of amber and jet, of glass or porcelain or ivory, of niello or of enamel. Chief of all these has been enamel. Enamel is really glass coloured with powdered oxides. Enamel is applied to the metal in the form of a moistened powder. When the article is heated the powder fuses and covers the surface with a glass-like glaze. Sometimes the pattern is *cut* into the surface in the form of little pits or depressions which are then filled with enamel. This is the champlevé method (French 'champlever'—to engrave). Sometimes the pattern is *built up* of little walls of metal ribbon soldered to the surface and the cells are then filled with enamel. This is cloisonné (French 'cloisonner'—to partition). Sometimes a whole surface is covered with enamel, it is then 'incrusted'. In addition to opaque enamel, some was translucent and permitted the colour of the metal or of the patterns beneath the enamel to gleam through.

When we consider a piece of jewellery, it is always well to think of the purpose for which it was made, otherwise, although it may be of lovely colour or form, or of exquisite workmanship, it will be meaningless. For the *head* there are crowns—kingly crowns and bridal crowns—with a host of coronets, diadems, tiaras and the like, there are combs, slides and pins, there are ear-rings, which are often most delightful pendants, and barbaric peoples have nose-rings. For the *neck* there are necklaces, collars and rings, there are chains in endless variety, often supporting lockets and pendants. The arms and fingers have bracelets, bangles and rings. Barbaric people have anklets. It will be noticed that the ring is easily of first importance, while the chain comes second. So far as *clothing* is concerned the brooch with the buckle which was formed from it takes first place, with a multitude of studs, buttons, hooks and links in rank or less importance.

It is an extraordinary fact that even at times when furniture and building were of the crudest kind, there was produced the most exquisite jewellery. In Britain, after the wonderful work of the Irish goldsmiths and of the British craftsmen in bronze, two sets of invaders came across the North Sea, each bringing their own distinctive form of jewellery. The Norsemen (Norse, Swedes and Danes) brought their interlaced animal patterns (*Plate XIII, 5*), while the Anglo-Saxons from the mouths of the Rhine and from the German-Danish shores brought a style used by the peoples of Europe from France to South Russia. These enriched their jewellery with garnets and other coloured stones, or with amber, set in deep pits in the gold or bronze (*Plate XIV*).

Until the end of the Wars of the Roses, England had very few periods of real peace. Life and possessions were insecure, and the only people who were permitted to wear jewellery, or who had money enough to pay for it, were the Nobles, and their chief interest was in weapons and armour. Only among the Clergy and in the Monasteries was there a possibility that articles of jewellery would be preserved, and not be thrown into the melting pot to meet the expenses of war, to pay ransoms and fines and the like. The supreme skill of the medieval metal worker is to be seen in the wonderful bishops' croziers that have survived.

The rather more settled and prosperous times of the Tudors, though they seem far from settled to us as we read of rebellions and revolts, saw a great increase in the demand for personal jewellery, especially of chains and rings. The portraits of Henry VIII and of Elizabeth simply glitter with jewels. The metalwork, although often exquisitely skilful, became more and more regarded as a setting for enamels and precious stones and so passes rather out of the scope of this reader, which deals with things in which the metalwork is the most important item (*Plates XIII, 2*).

THINGS TO DO

1. Every craftsman should seize every opportunity of adding to his knowledge of the material in which he works. Read all you can about 'gold' and 'silver'.

2. Continue adding to your notes about processes. Read up about 'gilding', 'plating', 'enamelling', 'engraving', etc.

3. Jewellery offers a wealth of sketching material. If your drawings are done on loose sheets, they can be filed in their correct order. This is best done

under three headings, (1) kind of article, (2) time, (3) place of origin. This will keep brooches separate from rings, etc.

4. The British Museum and the Victoria and Albert Museum. Handbooks and Guides give excellent information and illustrations about the jewellery of the Bronze and Early Iron Ages, etc. The Encyclopædia Britannica has plates and articles on Jewellery, etc.

5. Jewellers' windows are interesting to watch, although most of their wares are 'mass production'. Old copies of the 'Studio' magazine contain much excellent hand-made jewellery of recent make, some of it very lovely.

6. There are a number of simply written books on making jewellery on the market giving very clear directions. Copper is an excellent metal from which to make brooches. Discs, ovals, shield shapes, pierced designs can be very effective. A safety pin soldered on the back is an efficient fastening. Buckles can be made of copper or brass.

7. If a brazing hearth or an enamelling oven is available actual enamelling of small objects is possible. House buttons, brooches, buckles, hat or hair ornaments, pendants are among the things one can make.

(*b*) PLATE

WE have now to speak of PLATE, that is about articles made partly or wholly of the precious metals, and intended to serve some useful purpose. The two great groups of plate are connected in some way with eating or drinking.

Those concerned with *drinking* are mainly of one or two forms. In the first the part that holds the liquid is large and stands directly upon the table, or is raised upon a low base that is little more than a rim, or stands upon small feet. Included in this type are bowls, tumblers, mugs, flagons, tankards, beakers, jugs, pails, mazers, horns, etc. The other kind has the part which holds the liquid raised upon a stem which separates the base from the bowl, or else the base itself is continued upwards and serves as a stem. The chalice and the egg-cup may serve as examples. For small examples glass has largely taken the place of metal and the wine-*glass* has quite taken the place of the wine-*cup*. It was customary to speak of an intoxicated person as being 'in his cups'.

Those concerned with *food* are mainly in the shape of plates or dishes. Of other table articles, the Salts are perhaps the most interesting (*Plates XVI, XVIII*). They should *not* be called salt-cellars. They have nothing to do with cellars. Both 'salt' and 'cellar' mean the same thing, 'salt' being Anglo-Saxon, and 'cellar' being a Latin derivation nearly connected with the word 'salary' which was the salt-money paid as part of their wages to the Roman soldiers. When we say a man is worth his salt we really mean that he earns his wages.

Knives, forks and spoons form another interesting group.

Naturally there are other groups of articles made of the precious metals, of which candlesticks, or caskets, may be mentioned. The name '*plate*' given to these articles comes from the Latin 'plata' meaning a thin sheet. In Spanish 'plata' means silver.

Although articles of solid gold were made in the earliest days, silver slowly became the more common metal, and in the middle ages most plate was made of silver and gilded with gold leaf. When the surface was not wholly covered it was said to be part or 'parcel. gilt. After the discovery of America the 'Plate' fleets brought so much silver from the Spanish possessions that it became very common and was used for tables, mirror frames, etc.

The worker in precious metals was, however, usually referred to as a goldsmith, and this is illustrated by the fact that 'Goldsmith' is fairly common as a surname while 'Silversmith' is rare. So important a craft very soon organised itself for self-defence. As early as 1180 the Guild of Goldsmiths in London was fined by the King because it had not his licence to trade. It was so easy to cheat people with regard to the purity of gold or silver, or even to pass off worthless metal that had been gilded or silvered as if it were pure metal, that it was necessary to appoint someone who should certify the the quality of the metal used. At first King Henry III ordered the Mayor and Aldermen of London to select the six most 'discrete' goldsmiths to supervise the trade (in 1238). This was not enough, and so Edward I in 1300 ordered every silver vessel to be tested or 'assayed'. If it was up to the standard it was to be marked with the leopard's head. The testing goldsmiths were called 'guardiens' or wardens. As the testing took place in the Goldsmith's Hall the mark was called a 'hall mark'. We speak today of anything or any person not quite up to standard as being not up to the mark. The great day came in 1327 when Edward III gave the Goldsmiths full powers' Every Goldsmith was to have his own (trade) mark by which his work could be recognised and it was "ordained that all of the trade of goldsmith were to sit in their shops in the High Street Cheap" (that is, in the market of the High Street, or the present Cheapside) "and that no silver or gold plate ought to be sold in the City of London except in the King's Exchange or in Cheap . . . and that publicly, to the end that persons in the trade might inform themselves whether the seller came lawfully by it . . ." Because of this rule the Strand and Cheapside became a famous site for goldsmiths. In 1500 a high official of the Pope wrote home to Italy that all the shops of Milan, Rome, Venice and Florence put together could not equal the spectacle of the fifty-two goldsmiths in one street crowded with treasures of all sorts.

Neither gold nor silver is worked pure. They are both alloyed, silver mainly with copper, and gold mainly with silver. Silver had to conform to the standard set by the foreign merchants who traded in London by special Royal permission. These were mainly Dutch and German connected with the Hansa League. They came from the East and were called commonly 'Easterlings'. Their money was easterling or *sterling* money. Gold is reckoned by the 24th part called a 'carat'. Perfectly pure gold would be 24 carat. In the same way 22 carat gold means 22 parts pure gold and 2 parts alloy.

A study of plate reflects the manners and customs of people and tells of good and bad times, of the changes and chances of history. The best instance to take would be the drinking vessel. From the earliest days the horn was used. In Saxon days this was given metal 'mounts', rims, bands, and later on a cover or lid and feet. In the end of a horn being cut off and a metal base provided we have the beaker. Side by side with the *beaker* the wooden *bowl* was used. All forms of metal drinking vessels seem to have descended from one of these two.

When the beaker is given a foot and a stem it becomes a 'standing cup'. The utmost skill of the goldsmith was expended upon these. Every possible means of decoration was used. Exquisite examples have been preserved by the colleges of Oxford and Cambridge, by the Guilds and Companies of London, and among the 'plate' belonging to ancient towns (*Plate XVI*).

The drinking vessel made for use in the Church Service is an enthralling object for study. The Bible says that at the Last Supper, Christ took a cup and gave thanks, and handed it to His Disciples. Legend says that Joseph of Arimathea, who gave his sepulchre for the burial of Our Lord, fled from the Holy Land carrying the Cup with him, and landing in the West of England, lived at Glastonbury. The times became so evil that the Earth was no longer a fitting place for so holy a thing. It passed away, to be seen in visions only by the pure in heart. This was the Holy Grail. From the earliest days of Christianity until today a 'cup' takes its place in the most solemn of all Christian services. For many centuries this cup was in form a bowl raised on a stem and was called a chalice (*Plate XVIII*). This had (1) a bowl, (2) a stem with a swelling called (3) a knop to enable a firm hold to be taken, and (4) a foot. With the chalice there was used a metal plate (or paten) which was used (1) to cover the chalice, and (2) to carry the bread or wafer used in the Service. At first all the people drank from the chalice and it had a large bowl and sometimes two handles. Later on the Roman Catholic Church decided that the congregation should not drink from the bowl, but should have it shown to them, and so the bowl became very small. The shape of the foot changed as well. At first it was round. This caused the cup to roll when it was laid on its side to drain and so the foot was made with six or eight points. These tore the linen cloth and so the points were provided with rounded ends or projections.

These were likely to break off and so the base was lobed. A very small vessel, somewhat like a tiny coffee-pot was used to hold the wine before it was poured into the chalice. This was a cruet. This word comes from an old French word 'crue' which is related to our word 'crock' so that a cruet is just a small vessel. On our present day dining table the little containers are the cruets, and the holder is a cruet-stand.

Throughout the Middle Ages the wealth in plate of the Churches increased, mainly because they were not permitted to part with it, except for ransoming prisoners or in time of famine. We read that in order to pay the enormous ransom of Richard Cœur de Lion gold and silver chalices were handed up and shrines were stripped of their jewels and precious coverings.

Then came the Reformation. Everything that had been used in the services of the old Church was discarded. Its great wealth tempted King and people. It was stated of Edward VI that, "the Kinges Majestie has need presently of a masse of money". His own expenses, the cost of fortifications, of garrisons, of keeping the army, etc., all demanded money. Robbing the Church was not only easy, it was held to be almost a virtue. The Roman Catholic Church was regarded as an enemy by the Protestants. Under the reforming Bishops it became a crime to keep or use any vessel or article that had on it an image or an inscription. Any representation of the Cross or the Crucifixion was forbidden. Chalices might no longer be used. It was ordered that plain Communion *Cups* were to take their places. Elizabeth instructed that each church should possess "a ffaire and comely cup of sylver and cover of sylver". In some places the change was so sudden that suitable cups and vessels were taken from common use for service in the church. When silver was not obtainable, pewter was used. Sometimes the old chalices were handed to the goldsmiths to melt down and remake into the new plain Cup. A return was made to the old custom by which all the members of the congregation drank from the Cup, and so it was necessary to make the bowl large again. So that after the Reformation the Communion Cups had usually large bowls of the beaker type, they were either severely plain, or had a band of engraved 'arabesque' decoration, and they avoided the stem with its knop as being too much like the old chalice. In place of the tiny cruet, large tankards or flagons were used for holding the wine which were often exactly the same as those used in the homes and inns of the people.

It must not be thought that the few articles mentioned above were the only ones made by the goldsmith for the Church. There were very many others . . candlesticks, holders for sacred relics called monstrances, shrines, book and bell covers, basins, salvers, censers, and so on. There is no space here to speak of them.

In the same way there is no space to show how history is reflected in the work of gold and silver that was made for use outside the church. All that can be done is to give a short summary of the twelve periods into which the story can be divided. It must be remembered that the dates, especially the early ones, are not exact, and that, in some cases one period overlaps another for many years.

1. THE EARLY BRITISH. 1500 B.C.—200 A.D. This period covers work made both in Britain and in Ireland. The Roman Invasion interrupted work in England but not in Ireland. Among the objects made were lunulæ, collars, torcs, chains, brooches, sun-discs, bowls, armlets, pins, etc.

2. THE ROMAN PERIOD. 50 A.D.—400 A.D. The Roman invasion interrupted the native worker who, if he survived, probably fled to the west or to Ireland. Under the Romans metalwork was classical in design, i.e., copied from Greek or Roman work. (*Plate XV, 1*).

3. THE ANGLO-SAXON PERIOD. 400 A.D.—1050 A.D. The Anglo-Saxons brought with them a love of strong, brightly jemmed metalwork. When they became Christian they stopped burying precious or useful articles with their dead so that it is only by lucky chance that we have a few specimens of their work. They were masters of the kind of decoration called 'niello' (meaning 'black'). In this process the surface of the metal is hollowed out leaving the design in relief. The hollows are filled with a powder of silver, lead, copper, borax and sulphur which is fused by heat. This gives a rich black amalgam, and when the surface is polished the design stands out clearly.

4. THE IRISH MIDDLE AGE PERIOD. 900 A.D.—1200 A.D. During this time English history is a record of rebellion, invasions and bloodshed. In Ireland there was comparative peace. The church was strong, craftsmen were able to work safely. This was one of the wonder periods of metalworking. The very greatest authority, Sir C. J. Jackson, writes: "In considering examples of the art of the Keltic goldsmith, selected from objects mainly found in Ireland . . a style of ornamentation was evolved which . . appears *never to have been surpassed*. . It is an indisputable fact that in no country has there been found evidence of native work . . composed of various metals and enriched with enamels and inlays, which, for beauty of form and colour, as well as for skilful treatment of its most minute parts, *will bear comparison* with the Irish work . ." In the famous Ardagh Chalice (*Plate XIII*) there was used gold, silver, brass, copper and bronze, enamel work and set stones and amber, silver and gold filigree work of utmost delicacy, inlaid work and chased and punched decoration.

Among a wealth of surviving work are chalices, bell and gospel shrines, brooches, croziers and crosses. War and invasion put an end to this wonderful time. The Normans under Robert Strongbow, Earl of Pembroke, landed in 1169.

5. THE NORMAN PERIOD. 1100—1200. Very, very little remains of the art metalwork of this period. One glorious exception is the

PLATE XV

1. Two Roman Silver Dishes, ornamented with classical figures in repoussé work. Found at West Row, Suffolk, and now in the British Museum.

2. English eighteenth-century Sugar and Fruit Basins of pierced and decorated silver.

F

PLATE XVI

1. An English Communion Cup, Bell and Salt of the seventeenth century.

2 and 3. The Goldsmith's Cup and Richard Chester Cup : finely wrought English Renaissance standing cups.

'Gloucester candlestick' which looks like a last glorious work of the Anglo-Saxon craftsman.

6. THE GOTHIC OR MEDIEVAL PERIOD. 1200—1500. During this time the goldsmith was encouraged, first by the Church, and later by both Church and wealthy people. The wealth of Church plate has been mentioned. Outside the Church the Royalty, the Noble families, the rich Nobles, the Town Councils and the great Guilds turned much of their wealth into plate. A display of plate was the easiest way of indicating wealth. Special furniture, both permanent and portable was made to display the plate. In France, at one time, a person's rank was indicated by the number of shelves permitted on his 'dressoir' where his plate was 'dressed' or arranged for show. Plate could easily be carried from place to place, it could easily be melted down to pay ransoms or forced loans, it could easily be carried abroad if necessary in times of exile. Enormous quantities have been destroyed, but enough remains to show the variety, beauty and exquisite skill of the work. The main decoration followed the kind of architecture of the time.

7. THE RENAISSANCE PERIOD. 1500—1600. After the long Gothic period, a number of brief periods followed. The Renaissance was the first of these. There was increasing trade, increasing wealth, increasing security in towns, increasing comfort and luxury in the way the wealthy people lived. Plate became more ornate, and the simpler architectural designs gave place to a wealth of flowers, leaves and fruit, with Greek mouldings and Roman forms of decoration. Side by side with homely tankards and flagons, strange shaped ewers and Italian articles, such as 'tazzas' appeared. In contrast to this riot the Church in Britain lost its wealth and returned to plain Communion Cups, etc.

8. THE EARLY STUART AND COMMONWEALTH PERIOD. 1600 —1660. The glory of the Renaissance was short lived in England. The extravagance of the Sovereigns, the drain of war expenses, the bitter religious persecutions, the continual forced loans and heavy taxation all made the country poor. The plate became thinner and simpler in shape, and during the brief Commonwealth almost ceased to be made. It is a wonder that anything survived the Civil War.

9. THE LATE STUART PERIOD. 1660—1700. The shortest and most extraordinary period. The discovery of the silver mines in South America poured an apparently unlimited stream of silver into Europe. The rulers of Europe were practically dictators with small, privileged and very wealthy nobilities. The people were mainly poverty-stricken. In England Charles II wasted the country's money upon his favourites. In the palaces and houses of the wealthy plate was used as it had never been before. Candlesticks and candelabra, mirror frames, rose-water ewers and basins, huge wine-coolers and bowls, even tables and fire irons were made of silver. The fashion

spread and the Inns began to have displays of silver tankards. The demand for silver was so great that the coinage was clipped and even melted down until there was such a shortage that drastic laws were passed raising the purity of silver to be used in making plate so that the coinage silver could not be used. This almost stopped the making of plate except for very thin work which was decorated with designs of fruit and flowers in repoussé, which was a form of decoration that followed William and Mary from the Low Countries.

10. THE EARLY GEORGIAN OR ROCOCO PERIOD. 1725— 1765. With the coming of the Hanoverian monarchs England was at last free from the danger of civil war. Life and trade were secure. England offered a safe home to refugees from abroad and many skilful craftsmen from France settled in this country. These brought with them the strange style called rococo. This is based upon the use of broken curves and scrolls, and the shell is a common part of the decoration. A very great goldsmith called Paul Lamerie who was an exiled Huguenot worked in London in this style.

11. THE LATE GEORGIAN PERIOD. 1765—1830. This might be called the second renaissance. The discovery of the ruins of the Roman towns of Herculaneum in 1738 and of Pompeii in 1755 turned the thoughts and studies of artists and craftsmen to the work of ancient Rome and Greece. The metal-worker copied the forms of the Greek vase and other articles wherever he possibly could and used the Greek and Roman styles of decoration. It was during this period that a great deal of 'Sheffield Plate' was made. A Sheffield metalworker who made buttons and spurs, etc. discovered one day in 1743 as he was repairing a knife handle that silver would fuse with copper if they were heated. He was Thomas Boulsover (1704— 1788). He laid thin sheets of silver on thicker sheets of copper and after they had been fused together was able to beat them out to any required thinness, and to make small articles that resembled silver, but were copper inside. Other makers copied his method, except that they soon rolled the sheets instead of beating them, and practically every thing that was made in gold or silver was copied in Sheffield Plate.

12. THE VICTORIAN PERIOD AND AFTER. 1830—1930. At the end of the late Georgian period machinery was beginning to produce hundreds or even thousands of copies of the same 'model'. This made things cheap. The craftsman, in his workshop, working with hand tools, could not possibly make things so cheaply, and so he was driven out of work. It was a long time before an attempt was made to return to the old ways of making things. It is clear also that real hand-made things must be expensive. Today a great effort is being made to produce hand made articles in a style unlike the old styles. The new style is much simpler and depends more upon the shape of the article than upon its decoration for its attraction.

THINGS TO DO

1. Look up all words such as 'arabesque', 'monstrance', 'tazza', 'censer'.

2. There is much written about plate. Even if the writing is dull the illustrations are always worth looking at.

3. Draw and sketch as much as possible. Do not trouble too much about decoration. A true drawing of the *shape* comes first. A collection of careful drawings of the shapes of any single article of plate would always be valuable. The Chalice is perhaps the best to study.
Careful drawings of details follow the drawings of shapes. Be careful always to '*date*' as nearly as possible any drawing of plate.

4. Neither silver nor gold will be available, but copper is a most excellent substitute. Prepare careful drawings, based upon your sketches and drawings of old work, until you are fully satisfied that what you wish to make is (1) possible with the skill you have, (2) worth making, and you may avoid producing the ghastly stuff usually called 'art metalwork'. If you cannot design, copy faithfully old work.

5. Make haste slowly. Learn to use the hammer first . . then add the repoussé punches one by one. Practice on any odd scraps of metal. Do simple things well first. Many old salts in pewter and in Sheffield plate are excellent models for plain hammer work.

CHAPTER SEVEN

The Dinner Table

Of course jewellery and plate is not for common wear, nor for everyday use. The everyday things have as long and interesting a story, and many of these belong to the table and the fireside. We speak of the 'dinner' table because that is the ancestor of tables. The breakfast, tea, occasional and other tables are all descended from the dinner table.

We should remember that earthenware and articles such as bowls made of wood came before articles of metal and that the metal-worker copied at first from these things.

Almost everything on the table comes from one of four simple forms. These are the circular plate, the bowl, the pitcher and the beaker.

The *plate* has a distinguished story. It probably copied the wooden platters or trenchers of the Middle Ages, and it soon gave way to earthenware or china plates. Its larger form, the dish, was in use long ago. The Venerable Bede, writing of King Oswald in A.D. 65 that "when he was once sitting at dinner, on the holy day of Easter, with . . . a *silver dish* full of dainties before him and they were ready to bless the bread, the servant, whom he had appointed to relieve the poor, came in a sudden, and told the king, that a great multitude of needy persons from all parts were sitting in the streets begging some alms of the king, he immediately ordered the meat set before him to be carried to the poor, and the dish to be cut in pieces and divided among them".

Metal platters were square in shape first, and the ease with which metal can be hammered into any shape enabled oval dishes to be made, but it is surprising how the circular shape which reminds one of the potter's wheel or the turner's lathe persists with plates and dishes. The dish called a '*salver*' has a strange story. In the Middle Ages the risk of poisoning was great enough for Kings and Princes to keep 'tasters'. The portion tasted was placed on a salver, so called from a Latin word 'salvare' to save. (Salvage is stuff *saved* from a wreck.) In England the salver was introduced to save or prevent drops of beer or wine from spoiling the clothes of guests when servants were pouring out.

The *tray* probably evolved very early from the dish.

Bowls were primitive drinking vessels. They were of common use from Anglo-Saxon until Tudor times. Their use was continued when tea was first introduced. This was drunk from small bowls, as it still is in Japan. The common drinking bowl was wooden (or

PLATE XVII

1. English Silver Spoons of the fourteenth (*left*), fifteenth (*one from left*) and sixteenth centuries (*remainder*).

2. English Georgian Silver Spoons of 1765-1792. The design has altered little to the present day.

PLATE XVIII

1 and 2. Two medieval silver Communion Chalices, each with an ornamental 'knop' to enable a firm hold to be taken.

3 and 4. The Mostyn and Vyvyan Salts : highly decorated examples of English Renaissance craftsmanship.

treen ware) and was easily turned on the simplest pole lathe. It was unbreakable. The medieval wooden drinking bowl is now usually called a mazer. It was turned from bird's-eye maple, and the name means 'spotted'. The common bowls and cups were of beech wood. Well-to-do people had silver rims put on their mazers. The rim was sometimes very broad and was engraved with names or an inscription. Occasionally other silver bands were added, as well as silver feet. A few mazers were even raised upon stands, and so became standing cups. When a bowl is raised upon a foot and stem it becomes a chalice, or cup. Loving-cups have two or more handles. In the Middle Ages such curiosities as ostrich eggs, or coco nuts were often given silver mounts like cups of silver or gold.

As everyone knows, fingers were made, and used, before forks. In wealthy households the custom arose of page boys, or servants carrying scented or 'rose water' around during meals. This was poured over the fingers and caught in bowls or basins. An early book of manners, "The Lytle Children's Lytil Boke," (1480) said, "allow those more worthy to wash first and after having washed . . .refrain from spitting in the basin". Long years afterward, the basin came to almost every table in the shape of the sugar-basin.

Bowls of different sizes were used as salt holders from the earliest times. The finest of these were the marvellous 'master salts' made for the high tables. They had all kinds of shapes, some like chalices, some in shape of hour glasses, some purely fanciful (*Plate XVIII*). The famous Earl of Leicester had a "Salte ship fashion, of the mother of pearl, garnished with silver and divers workes of warlike engines and ornaments, with xvi pieces of ordnance, whereof ii of wheles, two archers on the fore parte, and on the stearne the image of Dame Fortune standing on a globe with a flag in her hand".

For actual use small trencher salts were made. Salt spoons were not made till the end of the seventeenth century. Before then the book of manners instructed that "salt be removed from the cellar with a clean knife and laid on the trencher."

The shape of the 'rose water' ewer was copied later on for sauce-boats, cream and milk jugs, etc.

The derivation of the *beaker* from the drinking horn has been mentioned already. The oldest metal beaker in England dates from 1346. Small metal beaker shapes are still used for measuring liquids. When in the Army the rum 'ration' or 'tot' was issued, or when in the Navy they 'splice the main-brace' a small metal beaker measure is used. When the beaker shape was raised upon a foot and stem it gave rise to the standing cup, upon which the highest skill of the goldsmith was often expended. If the beaker be inverted, the shape of the tankard or the flagon is obtained. These were probably copied from wooden drinking vessels made of staves. It was customary for a number to drink from the same tankard, and in order to make sure that each had the same amount, a number of small pegs were put down the inside of the vessel. Each drank from one peg to the next, so that when we speak of taking someone 'down a peg or two' we really use the language of our forefathers.

KNIVES, FORKS AND SPOONS. There is no need to mention the extreme antiquity of the knife. For centuries the knife was the only help man had at his meals. Spoons and forks were known to the Egyptians and Assyrians. The British Museum has also two Saxon forks, one silver, one of iron. It also has Saxon spoons. These, however are extreme exceptions. There are very few references to forks during the Middle Ages. They seem to have been used at Royal Courts for eating fruits, spiced ginger, etc. Not until Elizabeth's reign did the very wealthy begin to provide even knives for their guests. It was polite for the gentlemen to cut up the meat for the ladies. Both ladies and gentlemen, however, began to carry with them their own table knives, and beautiful cases were made for these 'case' or 'sheath' knives. James I has the distinction of naming the 'jack' knife, which was the first knife to close into its handle. The actual use of the fork at table came to England at this time from Italy. A book of the time states "the reason for this curiosity is because the Italians can not endure by any means to have his dish touched by fingers, seeing that all men's fingers are not alike clean."

The custom was laughed at, ridiculed, and even preached against as blasphemy, God having provided men with fingers, but the custom slowly gained way. Particular people carried with them delightful cases with a knife and fork, and to these a spoon was soon added. It was not until Queen Anne's days that the very wealthy began to supply their most important guests with a knife, fork and spoon. The forks had two prongs only until the eighteenth century, and carving forks still have but two. The fourth prong was added within the last forty years.

Spoons are very ancient. The Israelites made them, "and thou shalt make the spoons thereof of pure gold", we read in Exodus. From the time of the Normans until James I the stem was polygonal and ended in a 'knop'. The shape this knop takes is used to name the spoon. There are 'diamond points', maiden heads, acorns, seal heads (like seals for official use), etc. The best known are the Apostle spoons of which the whole set consisted of the Twelve Apostles and the Master Spoon, usually Our Lord. Sometimes St. Paul was added, while people who were not Apostles at all, such as Queen Elizabeth, Julius Cæsar, and King Arthur, were sometimes represented. Towards the end of this time the stem began to be flattened and the knop to be omitted. The end was 'slipped' or finished like a slanting cut. These were followed by perfectly plain ended puritan spoons which must have been awkward to hold. After the Restoration the end broadened in a variety of ways but this gradually took the very beautiful Old English style about 1750 and has remained much the same ever since (*Plate XVII*). The shape of the bowl and the method of joining this to the stem are interesting and should always be noted. Some old spoons have marrow scoops at the end of the stem. The introduction of Tea and Tea Caddies was followed by the making of delightful little caddy spoons. The discovery of new lands and the opening of new trade routes led to the introduction of new commodities. New foods and new drinks appeared on the tables and new articles of plate were made for their use. First came a better supply of spices and condiments. These were very welcome as it became possible to vary the great monotony of beer as a drink and salt meat as food. Pepper *casters* appeared, delightfully shaped and with a great variety of pierced heads. A caster is just a small container from which the contents are cast through a perforated head. Ale and wine was spiced and sweetened —first with molasses and then with sugar. Punch bowls and ladles were made, and caudle and posset cups. The latter were squat, full-bodied cups with lids and two handles. Caudle was a thin gruel with spiced and sweetened ale or wine. Possett was hot milk curdled with spiced and sweetened ale or wine. Sugar basins and sugar tongs were made (*Plate XV*). Trade with the East brought Coffee and then Tea to England. This introduced the Coffee-pot, the Teapot and delightful little Tea Caddies. Following these came cream and milk bowls and jugs, jugs for hot water, tea trays, stands for hot vessels, etc. The addition of mustard and of spiced sauces to the pepper and salt on the table brought the cruet-stand which is now generally called the cruet. These are only some of the metal articles that increase of trade has brought to our tables.

THINGS TO DO

1. Most of the articles mentioned in this section can be made, at any rate, in their simple forms, in an ordinary metalwork room, or at home with a limited set of tools. Draw old models. Fill your sketch book with the simple contour shapes of bowls, or of spoons. Many churches have good old brass alms or collecting dishes, and the repoussé work on them is worth studying.

2. Make series of drawings showing the evolution of present day drinking vessels from the drinking-horn; or of the vessels that have evolved from the simple wooden bowl.

3. A study of spoons is particularly interesting as it is possible to make many of the shapes. It is not at all difficult to electroplate copper articles. It is better not to attempt silver plating as the electrolyte is a cyanide, and is a deadly poison. Nickel is much better. The electrolyte should be made up as follows:

Nickel ammonium sulphate -	$1\frac{1}{2}$ oz.
Salammoniac - - -	$\frac{1}{4}$ oz.

Boric Acid - - - - $\frac{1}{4}$ oz.

Water - - - - - - 1 pint

The object to be plated *must* be absolutely clean of all dirt or grease. Get full directions from any good science book. Do not even handle with the fingers as the skin is always slightly greasy. After nickel plating the object will need *polishing* on a "Buffing wheel".

PLATE XIX

1. A Steel Grate at Brocket Hall, Hertfordshire, designed by James Paine (*circa* 1760).

2. English Silver Candlesticks of *circa* 1700.

PLATE XX

1 and 2. Early eighteenth-century brass Candelabra from the churches at Wymondham, Norfolk and Northiam, Sussex.

3 and 4. Brass Lecterns of the fifteenth century from Norfolk and Bristol.

CHAPTER EIGHT

Lighting and Heating

IN providing the light and heat for our homes, many metalworkers, the blacksmith, the gold and silversmith, the coppersmith, the pewterer and brassfounder, have all taken a hand.

The first act of Creation records, "And God said, Let there be light, and there was light". The great gulf between man and the beast is marked by man's control of fire. The origin of fire is always regarded as divine in the old myths. Prometheus, the legend tells, stole fire from Heaven, and gave it to man. In many parts of the Earth, fire-worship or sun-worship has been practiced. Fire for the lighting of caves and huts and for safety against the wild beast, fire for its life giving and life preserving warmth, fire for the cooking of food and the hardening of spear points, fire for the miraculous extraction and working of metals, fire for the innumerable purposes of man, all these raise a study of the articles used for the control of light and fire above the ordinary level.

The oldest *lamps* in Britain are probably the hollowed blocks of chalk found in the flint mines of Cissbury in Sussex, where prehistoric man mined with deer antlers for flint. One cannot be sure where or when metal lamps were first made. The development of the lamp and of the candlestick seems to have gone on side by side. 'Lamp' comes from an old Greek word meaning a 'torch', while 'candle' comes from a Roman word meaning a 'white light' such as that given from wax or tallow. There must have been a long story of lamps of bronze and other metals before the metalworkers could produce such a candlestick as is described in the 25th Chapter of Exodus, "And thou shalt make a candlestick of pure gold: of beaten work shall the candlestick be made : his shaft, and his branches, his bowls, his knops, and his flowers shall be the same. And six branches shall come out of the sides of it, three branches of the candlestick out of the one side, and three branches of the candlestick out of the other side; three bowls made like unto almonds, with a knop and a flower in one branch: and three bowls made like unto almonds in the other branch with a knop and a flower: so in the six branches that come out of the candlestick . . . all of it shall be one beaten work of pure gold".

This wonderful candlestick was accompanied by lamps, for the writer continues, "And thou shalt make seven lamps . . . and the tongs thereof and the snuff-dishes thereof shall be of pure gold".

When Solomon rebuilt the Temple he had many candlesticks and lamps made of pure gold, and these were carried in triumph in Rome after Titus had taken Jerusalem in 70 A.D. Candles and candlesticks are mentioned in the Bible from Job—which is regarded by many as being the oldest book of all—to Revelations where the Seven Churches in Asia are referred to as seven golden candlesticks. Christ makes delightful mention of candles in the parables. The most striking incident in the old Excommunication service was when the priest extinguished a candle as showing the blotting out of the soul of the excommunicated person. The burning of candles in churches or before shrines as the symbol of prayer rising to God or as a sacrifice of remembrance is well known. One of the special Services of the old Church was called Candlemas, on Feb. 2nd when the candles for the year were consecrated. Candles are still used for lighting churches. The famous Chapel of King's College in Cambridge is so lighted.

Metal devices for holding candles are numerous. When suspended from the ceiling this is called a *chandelier*. The simplest form and perhaps the earliest type was the suspended hoop. The candles were pressed down upon points or 'prickets' around the circumference. Sometimes, in place of the hoop, two arms were crossed at right-angles. In Elizabeth's time the first chandeliers of crystal or cut glass were imported from Italy. The first of all are preserved at Penshurst in Kent. These developed into enormous chandeliers of cut glass in the early days of Queen Victoria. When William and Mary came from Holland, chandeliers of brass became common. The distinguishing feature is the large brass ball from which the arms spring. Many of these are to be seen in churches and there is an extremely large one in the Victoria and Albert Museum (*Plate XX*).

CANDLESTICK is the usual name for a standing support for one candle. The first candlestick was probably no more than a pointed wooden stick. When there are more candles than one the holder is commonly called a CANDELABRUM. In Greek and Roman days the candelabrum was a tall metal lampstand in the form of a pillar or fluted column which was usually supported upon three spreading legs of animal form. In some Christian churches there are huge standing candlesticks. One of the most wonderful of these is now in Milan Cathedral. It is of gilt bronze and is more than 14 feet high. It is thought to be the finest piece of metalwork made in the thirteenth century. Both pricket and socket candlesticks have been made from Roman times. The favoured metal through the Middle Ages in England seems to have been brass. After the reign of Charles II, silver became more common, and a very great number were made of Sheffield Plate (*Plate XIX*). For ordinary domestic use, iron, pewter, brass, and sometimes copper were used. As might be expected, peasant craftsmen in many countries made candlesticks, usually of iron, both for themselves and for their friends. A common form held three candles and by some was supposed to represent the Holy Trinity.

During the twelfth and thirteenth centuries at Limoges in France, much very beautiful enamelled work on copper was made and among the articles were candlesticks, often very delightful in shape and colour. Wall brackets for candles were made from the time of Charles the Second and these were often provided with polished reflectors, or often were placed beside mirrors. Some very lovely brass candle-brackets may still be seen on old pianos. The ancient classic nations developed the lamp that took its perfected form under the Greeks in the shape that is commonly called an 'Aladdin' lamp (*not* the modern commercial article of that name). During the Middle Ages and down to very recent times lamps were quite disused until the introduction of cheap paraffin was followed by the 'oil' lamp—standing, hanging and bracket.

For outdoor lighting, torches or links vied with lanterns. Even today there are still to be seen in London a very few of the wrought iron link-holders and extinguishers that once were common outside important houses (*Plate X*). And here and there, there remain the wrought iron brackets from which lanterns were hung for lighting streets. The tall metal standards that now serve in our street lighting are useful but usually are *not* beautiful.

A whole chapter might be written about the connection between metalwork and the hearth or fireplace. First come the fireirons themselves, the poker, tongs and shovel. These lead our thoughts to the tools used by the smith in his work, and then on to all those tools and appliances by means of which man has used heat in his craft work. Then one thinks of the innumerable array of appliances and vessels used for cooking, the cauldrons, skillets, saucepans, kettles, pans and dishes, the scoops, ladles, forks, the toasting forks, spits and their mechanism, the stands, racks, cranes, tripods and trivets, the firedogs, andirons, firebacks, grates, firebuckets, kerbs, stoves, ranges, ovens, etc., and one gets some idea of the claims made by the hearth upon the metalworker. The list is by no means complete, and might be extended to include braziers and the well-known warming pans. All these things are interesting because their shapes depend entirely upon their purpose, and for many of them any attempt at decoration would be wasted energy. A few, however, such as the firedogs or andirons upon which the burning logs rested, and the firebacks which kept the burning logs from falling too far back on the hearth, were decorated. When coal took the place of logs, and the smaller 'fire place' supplanted the open hearth, very considerable attention was paid to the artistic designing of grates and stoves. Some of these, especially those designed at the time of the Adam Brothers were really fine pieces of work, and were supplied with 'fenders' and with chimney-pieces in the same style (*Plate XIX*). Nowadays there is a tendency to revert to the old plan of the hearth fire, and to use metal for hot water radiators and for gas or electric fires which certainly are at last becoming more pleasant to look at although very few indeed—if any—have any connection with hand work.

THINGS TO DO

1. The things to do here are mainly a continuance of things already started. For instance, Prometheus will be added to the list of persons looked up, Cissbury, Limoges, Penshurst will add to the list of places identified, while added to your list of new words may be such as 'links', 'skillets', 'trivets' etc.

2. The sketch book may be kept very busy in connection with this section . . . 'candlesticks' form a most delightful study, while many other of the objects are almost as good. Above all, make drawings of such things as lantern brackets, etc., that are in danger of destruction.

4. Very many of the objects mentioned may easily be made in the metal room . . candlesticks, candelabra, fire irons, toasting forks, trivets, hall lamps.

5. Many museums now have representations of old interiors and these almost always centre round the fire place. The Welsh National Museum at Cardiff, The Stranger's Hall at Norwich are just two of these. There is a wonderful museum of old Sussex ironwork at Lewes. Never miss an opportunity of seeing old work.

CHAPTER NINE

Odds and Ends

(*a*) THE PEWTERER

PEWTER is an alloy. Its principal ingredient is tin, and in some
pewter there is as much tin as there is gold in a sovereign. Tin
is a soft metal and needs some admixture to make it hard enough
for everyday use. The addition of a little copper makes a very hard
pewter. The highest grade pewter today is tin with a little copper
and antimony. This has a very bright silvery lustre. A common
coarse pewter is formed by mixing more or less lead with the tin.
The pewter sold today in the jeweller's shops usually has the label
'guaranteed to contain no lead'. Pewter has a low melting point and
so is not easy to solder. To get over this trouble a hard kind of
pewter was made during Victoria's reign called Britannia metal.
This, however, does not take the delightful soft lustre that pewter has
when polished. Apart from the fact that pewter is not easy to solder,
its softness prevents it from being beaten into thin sheets, or drawn
into wire, or decorated by repoussé. Pewter *can* be soldered if care is
taken not to overheat the iron, or, better still, it can be 'burned'
together. By this method a thin strip of the metal is laid over the
joint and by careful use of the iron it is fused and runs into the joint.
This is then cleaned up and the result should be a perfect and
invisible joint.

Pewter ware is made in three ways. Very much is cast, in which
case brass or gunmetal moulds are used, some is beaten; the difficulty
of working the metal keeps the beaten article to simple shapes and
simple ornament. English pewter is almost without decoration, and
so the *shape* becomes very important. Continental pewter is often
highly decorated with cast designs. The third method of making is
to spin the metal, that is, to put a sheet of pewter in a lathe and to
press it into shape with smooth ended tools while it is revolving
rapidly.

There is no certain knowledge as to when or where pewter was
first made. The Chinese appear to have used it at least 2,000 years
ago. The oldest piece of pewter in England is a Roman cup which
was made most likely between 380 and 400 A.D. We know that
there was a 'Worshipful Company' of Pewterers in London in 1348,
one year after the battle of Crecy. They were careful that their work
should be the best possible, and one of their rules forbade night work
because the bad light—there were only hand made tallow candles—
prevented good workmanship. It read, "Also the goodefolk of the
craft . . . ben acorded that non be so hardi to wirk ny nyght no
werk of peautre be cause it is regarded among thaym that the vew

of the night is not so profitable ne certen as it is of the day to the commen profit".

Tin has never been a common metal and pewter was expensive at least till Shakespeare's times. It was cheaper than silver, and churches that could not afford to buy chalices of silver were permitted to use pewter. Bishops and the clergy had commonly a pewter chalice and paten buried with them. In Edward VI's reign the London pewterers were granted the much prized 'right of assay' that is, they were given the duty of testing all pewter articles to make sure they were of the right quality. Pewter that was 'not up to the mark' could be confiscated, and was stamped with a *broad arrow* before it could be sold. So very much of the valuable plate belonging to the church was taken at the time of the Reformation, that many churches had to be content with pewter Communion cups, etc. In well-to-do families up to the time of Elizabeth pewter was used at the 'high' table in the place of 'treen' (or wooden ware) that was used by the servants in the Hall. The pewter was made in sets of twelve dishes, twelve platters and twelve saucers, each set being called a garnish. 'Garnish' really means 'to provide', and the food provided was offered upon the dishes, etc. The food provided by the kitchen for the 'high' table was prepared carefully and 'decked out' on the pewter service, so that 'to garnish' came to mean to decorate. When larger pewter articles were required for high days and holidays, larger dishes, etc. were hired from the makers. Later on flagons and tankards became very common and during the 17th century pewter was very widely used. Some of the articles made were flagons, tankards, salts (both large and small), peppers, beakers, candlesticks, candelabra, plates, dishes, bowls, vases, porringers, measures, ink-stands, salvers, bleeding basins (these were often hung outside the barbers' shops as business signs), patens, sugar bowls (*Plate XXII*). The introduction of cheap glazed earthenware in the 18th century led to the disappearance of pewter from the home. Earthenware was cheaper and did not need polishing. Pewter was still used in public houses and inns until glass became so cheap. The use of glass made it unnecessary for these places to keep a 'pot-man' whose main duty had been to clean the pewter. A cheap and very hard pewter was used until quite recently in the making of the milk-cans in which the milk was delivered from the dairies.

(b) Lead

This metal was known in ancient times. It is mentioned in the Book of Job, where Job wishes that his words were graven in the rock with lead for ever. This use of lead has persisted until today, for the inscriptions in gravestones are frequently filled with lead. In the British Museum there is a weight which is filled with lead. It was probably made by a Phœnician settler in Assyria sometime between 750 - 700 B.C. Again, this practice is followed today. Much has survived to show the considerable use made by the Romans of this metal. Cisterns, cups, water-pipes, weights are to be seen in museums. The worker in lead still retains a Latin name—he is a plumber—and the Latin for lead is plumbium. This also explains the name 'plumb line', the weighted line that builders use.

The softness of lead prevents it being decorated very much, but it can be cast and beaten. It was used in England, mainly in Norman times, in making fonts. Later on the heads of water-pipes were decorated (*Plate XXI*). Because of its power of resisting the weather lead has always been used for cast ornaments in gardens and upon gate pillars although its dull colour prevents a very wide use in this way, and now, as always, its chief use is in the way the plumber employs it, for roofing and piping.

(*c*) THE COPPERSMITH

The making of copper articles, and the extreme antiquity of copper has already been mentioned in several places. It is difficult to say how ancient the craft of the coppersmith is. Copper is a beautiful metal. It can be beaten, or cast, or drawn into wire. It can be worked in almost every possible way. It has the drawback that it oxidises to a green and poisonous verdigris. This, however, is turned to good account when roofs are covered with a copper sheeting. The green colour is very lovely when seen at a distance, and it also prevents any further oxidising, so that a copper sheeted roof is very lasting. For decorative purposes copper requires constant polishing, and for domestic purposes it is not safe in connection with food. For this reason copper articles are usually 'tinned' inside. The fact that copper conducts heat so well accounts for its use in coppers, urns, kettles and warming pans and for soldering-irons, while its use in the electrical industry is well known. When copper is alloyed with zinc it becomes *brass* which is a metal that resists rust. One thinks immediately of the use of brass in the making of musical instruments, of 'the sounding brass and tinkling cymbals' of the Bible down to the Brass bands of today. The esteem with which people regarded brass in the olden days is shown by the many references to that metal in the Bible. Both the cloudless sky and the parched earth during times of drought are spoken of as being like brass. The strength of brass supplies the saying 'his bones are as stong pieces of brass'. The work of the brassfounder is mentioned often in Exodus in the commands for the making of the Tabernacle, such as, 'thou shalt cast five sockets of brass,' etc. Brass was beaten into thin sheets for covering wooden articles. Samson was bound with fetters of brass. Goliath had a helmet, shield and greaves of brass. The following brazen articles are mentioned in the Old Testament: taches (metal tassels on the ends of curtain cords), lavers (shallow basins), altars, pillars, bases of pillars, chapiters (capitals of pillars), pins, rings, pots and shovels of bright brass, cymbals, gates, vessels of brass (these made for temple use are mentioned many times), censers, wheels. The use of brass in the making of idols is referred to more than once, and all know of the 'brazen serpent.' Solomon sent especially to Tyre for a skilful worker in brass named Hiram, and his wonderful work is described in detail in the two Books of the Kings. The continued use of brass in the Temple at Jerusalem is carried on in Christian churches today, for candlesticks are still most commonly made of brass, as well as lecterns, Collection plates, Alms dishes, etc. Another most interesting use of this metal has been in the making of memorial BRASSES which are to be found in many old churches. The carving of images of stone or wood in memory of famous people has never died out. These, however, are not only costly, but they take a great deal of space. When a small parish church is used as a burial place for many generations it is quite clear that it could not hold many monuments. This difficulty was got over very early indeed by the use of 'brasses' engraved with the figure of the deceased persons (*Plate XXI*). The very earliest brass known is of a bishop who died in 1231. The earliest brass in England is of the knight, Sir John Daubernoun in the Surrey Church of Stoke d'Abernon. Its date is 1277. Another very early brass is that of Sir Roger de Trumpington (1289) in Trumpington Church near Cambridge.

In the Middle Ages the brass used was always called 'latten' and for a long time was made round about Cologne and was imported through the East Coast ports. The sheets at first were thick, heavy and small in size. But later on very large sheets were made. Many of the early brasses were richly enamelled, but enamel does not expand or contract as the brass does with heat or cold, and so it cracks, works loose, and comes away. These brasses are of the greatest value. They show us the exact dresses of all classes of people throughout a great part of our history, the clothes of Knights and ladies, of bishops and priests of all kinds, of lawyers and merchants, of judges and doctors, of children and young people as well as of grown-ups, they show us the styles of hairdressing, they give us a complete picture book of armour. They are especially valuable because they are mostly dated, or they can be dated exactly because of the people they represent. On many of the brasses the lettering is very beautifully engraved. It is surprising that we do not know anything about the craftsmen who engraved the brasses; there must have been most skilful draughtsmen as well as highly trained engravers. It is thought that in some cases the brasses were produced by bell-founders.

Mention should also be made here of the beautiful brass lecterns, usually, in the form of eagles with wings outspread, which are often to be found in medieval churches (*Plate XX*).

Engraving metal for decoration led to one of the most surprising results. We have spoken of the method of filling engraved designs with a black compound, the result being called niello work. The goldsmiths of Florence in Italy brought this style to great perfection; in order to see how their engraving was proceeding they took prints of their work at intervals. Some people think that these prints

PLATE XXI

1. An eighteenth-century lead Rainwater head at Shrewsbury.

2. The "Free Miner" Brass at Newland Church, Gloucestershire.

3. An English lead Cistern of 1735 decorated with designs of Flemish origin.

PLATE XXII

1. A French pewter Porringer and Cover of the early eighteenth century.

2. An English pewter Plateau of 1662 ornamented with the royal arms.

suggested the making of engraved plates for printing many copies. Germany however was the first country to produce 'engravings' from metal plates, although after a start had been made, probably about 1450, both Italy and Germany led the new craft for many years. Even if the work of the goldsmith did not give the suggestion for printing engraving, the exquisite *skill* that the engraver had acquired was ready to be used, and the prints of the early engravers are masterpieces of art. The metal plate used was copper and the perfect skill with which inscriptions were cut for reproduction gave the name 'copper plate' to the beautiful style of writing that was taught by the 'Writing Masters' in schools. The finest of all engravers was a German named Albert (or in its German form 'Albrecht) Dürer (1471-1528). Not only was this great artist supreme in line engraving, but he also has the distinction of being the first to use the process called 'etching'. For an engraving the lines are scored or cut in the metal with a tool called a burin. For an etching the drawing is made by a needle scrathing through a thin film of wax on the metal surface. The metal plate is then placed in an acid bath and the acid eats the metal away from the exposed lines. The famous Dutch painter Rembrandt was probably the finest etcher who has ever lived. Other methods have been devised of printing from metal plates, and all the illustrations of this book have been produced from metal 'blocks'.

Neither should it be forgotten that metal very soon became the material from which printer's type was made, and when a new style is required today, after it has been designed, the first 'fount' or alphabet is cut in metal by hand.

And so ends, as Shakespeare says, "this strange, eventful history".

THINGS TO DO

1. Look back, through the book, to the 'things to do' and see whether any of them apply as well to something in this section.

   (*a*) Some of the metals may not have been mentioned before. They should be looked up wherever possible and every important detail noted.

   (*b*) Revise the list of greatmetal workers and add to the list the names of Dürer and Rembrandt.

   (*c*) Revise your list of words that were new to you, and add to them such words as 'treen', 'garnish', 'salver', 'latten or latton', etc.

   (*d*) Revise your notes of new processes and add notes on 'burning' joints, 'tinning' domestic articles, 'engraving', 'etching'.

2. Sheet pewter can be obtained, and if at all possible, the metal work student should beat up a few simple shapes, copying old models. Have nothing whatever to do with the thin foil pewter recommended for school use or for ladies' art classes. If a lathe is available try your hand at 'spinning' a simple plate or bowl. You will need to turn your wooden form first.

3. If there are any 'brasses' in the neighbouring churches an effort should certainly be made to take a rubbing or two. Remember that permission is necessary first from the vicar or rector. Cheap white 'lining' paper can be had from any wallpaper shop from 1s. a roll. Black heel-ball costs not more than 6d. a stick from a boot repairer.

4. Copper plate etching is quite possible if there is a press available for the printing. Simple book plates are as good as anything on which to experiment. Perfect your design in black and white first. Experiment in order to know how long to leave your plate in the acid, and do not be disappointed if your first efforts are failures.

INDEX

The Numerals in Roman characters refer to the plate numbers of illustrations.